# THE EVERYTHING

# WEDDING ETIQUETTE BOOK
*4th Edition*

Dear Reader,

Congratulations on your engagement! Now get ready to enter the wonderful whirlwind of wedding planning! Just wait—you'll have visions of cakes and gowns and diamonds dancing in your head (no matter how much you try to stop them!).

It really doesn't matter how many weddings you have attended or how many times you have been a bridesmaid; it's a very different story when you are the bride. The glory and the drama are all yours. Trivial details are not so trivial, a flower is not just a flower, and you now realize, yes, there are 100 shades of white— and you can tell the difference between them.

As a wedding planner, I have seen too many brides dwell on the what-ifs and doubt their choices amidst the din of others' opinions. For those brides, planning a wedding became a growing source of anxiety, and all the time and money spent planning a beautiful day didn't buy them the experience of really enjoying it.

The key is to keep it in perspective and remember that at the end of the day, the ultimate goal is to be married to the one you love,

Happy planning!

*Holly Lefevre*

# The EVERYTHING Series

These handy, accessible books give you all you need to tackle a difficult project, gain a new hobby, or even brush up on something you learned back in school but have since forgotten. You can read from cover to cover or just pick out information from our four useful boxes.

 **Alerts:** Urgent warnings

 **Essentials:** Quick handy tips

 **Facts:** Important snippets of information

 **Questions:** Answers to common questions

When you're done reading, you can finally say you know **EVERYTHING**®!

**PUBLISHER** Karen Cooper
**MANAGING EDITOR, EVERYTHING® SERIES** Lisa Laing
**COPY CHIEF** Casey Ebert
**ACQUISITIONS EDITOR** Lisa Laing
**SENIOR DEVELOPMENT EDITOR** Brett Palana-Shanahan
**EVERYTHING® SERIES COVER DESIGNER** Erin Alexander

Visit the entire Everything® series at *www.everything.com*

# THE EVERYTHING

# *Wedding*

# ETIQUETTE BOOK

*4th Edition*

From invites to thank-you notes—all you need
to handle even the *stickiest* situations with ease

Holly Lefevre

Avon, Massachusetts

*For Joe and Jules—I can't wait to plan your weddings!*

•   •   •   •   •   •

An Everything® Series Book.
Everything® and everything.com® are
registered trademarks of F+W Media, Inc.

Published by
Adams Media, a division of F+W Media, Inc.
57 Littlefield Street, Avon, MA 02322. U.S.A.
*www.adamsmedia.com*

ISBN 10: 1-4405-6151-6
ISBN 13: 978-1-4405-6151-1
eISBN 10: 1-4405-6152-4
eISBN 13: 978-1-4405-6152-8

Printed in the United States of America.

10  9  8  7  6  5  4  3  2  1

*This book is available at quantity discounts for bulk purchases.
For information, please call 1-800-289-0963.*

# Acknowledgments

I would like to thank the following people whose encouragement, insight, and guidance made this book possible: Amberly Finarelli and Andrea Hurst at Andrea Hurst Literary Management for bringing this project to me; Lisa Laing at Adams Media; Melissa Allen, director of catering and special events at the Ebell of Los Angeles, for her creativity and advice; Cynthia Adkins of A Legendary Affair; Patty Anderson; Christine Cudanes; Mary Sushinski of Occasions Bridal Consulting and Event Design; April Whitney of April Whitney Events; and, of course my husband, Brett.

## TOP TEN THINGS A GRACIOUS BRIDE KNOWS

1. Others may not know proper etiquette, but that doesn't mean you should ignore it.
2. Be humble. You may be a bride now, but soon you will re-enter life as a mere mortal.
3. Respect tradition, but give it your own personal spin.
4. Mind your manners. "Please" and "thank you" will take you a long way.
5. Your friends and family do not work for you but are happy to help you because they love you.
6. Don't assume anything. Ask questions and get the details in writing.
7. Don't keep guests waiting and don't ask them to pay for anything.
8. Treat your vendors kindly and they will do the same for you.
9. Thank-you notes are a must. It is never wrong to express your thanks to your parents, your guests, and your vendors.
10. If it doesn't feel right, don't do it. When in doubt, trust yourself.

# Contents

# Introduction

Trying on gowns, tasting cakes, breaking open the bubbly—talk about the time of your life! Go ahead and enjoy. Dive into that stack of bridal magazines and hop on the web to surf every fantastic wedding website—but remember you will eventually have to come to terms with the realities of wedding planning.

Planning a wedding can be a little overwhelming and slightly perplexing. Not only do you have a hundred different things to worry about, but your mother, future mother-in-law, and just about everyone you know is probably trying to tell you the right and wrong way to do things. Everyone, it seems, is an expert on weddings. So what's a well-meaning bride to do? If you've never planned a wedding, how can you be expected to know what is and isn't proper? Even if you have planned a wedding before, the definition of proper may be quite different than it was the first time.

Armed with the right information, you have the opportunity to take control of your wedding and the challenges that come with it. You can steer clear of the faux pas that have plagued so many brides. You can avoid the trap of doing things just because you think it is expected or because you think it must be okay if someone else did it. There's no need to rely on maybes and what-ifs when the dos and don'ts of proper wedding etiquette are at your fingertips.

How do you determine what is proper? The basic principle of etiquette can be summed up simply as the idea of not offending, nbarrassing, or upsetting others. While many questions of tiquette are simply a matter of common sense, other situations can be dealt with through consideration, communication, and a little kindness.

Marrying the complexities of wedding planning with the graciousness of etiquette is where *The Everything® Wedding Etiquette Book* comes in. This book will tell you how to solve contemporary etiquette dilemmas through practical advice while answering some of the most commonly asked wedding etiquette questions. Most importantly, this book recognizes that the world is an ever-changing place and that there are no hard and fast rules of etiquette anymore—what's right for one bride may not be right for another. Many questions, especially those dealing with today's complicated family dynamics, have no single correct answer; solutions to these types of dilemmas depend upon the particulars of each situation.

Throughout *The Everything® Wedding Etiquette Book*, the different aspects of planning and etiquette will be addressed with modern advice and answers that make sense in today's world. This guide also pays attention to traditional etiquette so that even your grandmother will be happy. While it is designed to relieve some of the stress associated with wedding planning, it will also give you advice and insights on how to plan a fabulous wedding. Within these pages you will find the answers to any type of etiquette dilemma you and your fiancé may face. Keep this book handy and you'll have the proper tools for dealing with any challenges that may come your way.

Congratulations, good luck, and enjoy!

CHAPTER 1

# THE Question

"*W*ill you marry me?" Did you have any idea how quickly your life would be transformed when you were asked THE question? Visions of cakes, dresses, and champagne flutes are dancing in your head—a true sign that you are now a bride-to-be! Soon after announcing your wonderful news, you are setting a date, registering for gifts, and attending your engagement party. It is a whirlwind of activity, and quite possibly one of the most fun and fabulous times of your life.

## The Proposal

An inspired proposal makes a great lifelong memory and begins your amazing wedding adventure. When it comes to asking for a hand in marriage, getting down on bended knee is "so yesterday." Popping the question is a creative endeavor; airplane banners, billboards, radio dedications, webcasts, television commercials, and even scavenger hunts are the new norm. However, traditionalists need not be intimidated. Heartfelt words, poems, and love letters never go out of style.

### Who Should Ask?

**My boyfriend has hinted that he wants to get married, and he's even been ring shopping, but he still has not proposed. Can I propose to him?** You can certainly propose to him. Just be prepared; if he is a traditionalist, it may take him some time to just to the role reversal. Ultimately you know your fiancé well enough to anticipate his reaction, and if you are comfortable and confident with popping the question yourself, go for it! However, if you think he has been ring shopping, he may already have some plans in the works, so your patience may pay off.

## Permission, Please

**My fiancé and I agreed to get married before talking it over with my parents. Will they be upset that he didn't consult them before proposing?** In this day and age it is highly unusual for parents to frown on a man's failure to ask for their daughter's hand in marriage. However, you know your parents better than anyone else, and if they are the traditional type, you may have some explaining to do. Generally if your parents are informed of the engagement promptly after the proposal, there should be no hard feelings.

## A Piece of the Rock

Oh, the ring! You have dreamed about it, looked for it, and waited for it. It is amazing how such a "little" thing can have such a huge impact on your life. Just like all the other facets of a wedding, with the ring come myriad questions, ideas, and expectations. You must research the options to make an informed decision about this important purchase.

### The Engagement Ring

**How do I go about making sure that I get the ring I want without appearing as if the ring is the most important part of the engagement?** Many men put a great deal of effort into the quest for an engagement ring, so your best bet is to discuss the matter openly with your fiancé, making him aware of your concerns. Explain how important it is that you find a good ring,

since it will be your most treasured possession. No doubt, h
quickly realize that your emphasis on this major purchase is we
warranted.

 **Alert**

An engagement ring is a major investment and a valuable piece of jewelry. In order to protect this investment from any sort of loss, be sure to contact your homeowners or renters insurance company and have the ring added to your policy right away.

**How much should an engagement ring cost?** There is the modern myth that the cost of a ring should equal two months' salary. The truth is some couples have an open-ended budget for the ring and others are just happy to have any ring. What is important is what the ring means to you and to your fiancé, not its price tag. An engagement ring should not cost more than you and your future spouse can afford to spend.

## Beyond a Diamond

**Can I wear a family heirloom as my engagement ring?** Wearing a family heirloom is a wonderful way to preserve the memory of a beloved family member or carry on a family tradition. The ring may come from either your fiancé's side of the family or your own.

**My fiancé gave me an engagement ring with an emerald stone. Doesn't the engagement ring need to be a diamond?** Although diamonds are the most popular choice for engagement rings, they are by no means the only acceptable alternative. Designs with or without precious stones are all acceptable options for an engagement ring.

## ...ng Dilemmas

**...nave a beautiful ring from my first marriage. Can I wear .hat as my engagement ring?** In a word, NO! Wearing the rings that were part of a marriage to someone else is insensitive and in very poor taste. If you have children from the previous marriage, put the ring aside for them or have the stone reset into a necklace or another piece of jewelry.

**I would prefer to wear my engagement ring as a wedding ring once we are married. Is it absolutely necessary to have two rings?** Many rings have unique designs that stand on their own, so wearing your engagement ring as a wedding ring is a very viable option. Prior to the wedding day, have the ring cleaned so it sparkles like new. Then pass it to the best man before the ceremony.

 **Essential**

In today's world, an engagement and an engagement ring generally go hand-in-hand. The truth is you can be engaged without a ring now, or ever. An engagement is a promise to marry. The ring has come to symbolize that promise, but it is not a requirement.

**Can I wear my engagement ring during the wedding ceremony?** You can. Simply slip your engagement ring on your right hand, and following the ceremony, slip it back onto your left hand, above the wedding ring.

## Wedding Rings

**Who traditionally pays for the wedding bands?** Traditional etiquette says the bride and/or her family should pay for the

groom's wedding band, and the groom and/or his family shou.
pay for the bride's wedding band

**Do our wedding bands have to match exactly?** Although many couples today wear matching wedding bands, there is absolutely no rule to this effect. It really all plays into your sense of style. As a little something special, many couples choose to engrave the inside of their bands with their initials and the date of their wedding.

**Once we're married, should the wedding rings be worn at all times?** Simply put, yes, although athletics, chores, and sometimes your job may call for you to take the ring off temporarily.

## Family Matters

You may want to share your good news with the world, but don't. Not yet anyway. Your families, your best friend, and any children or possibly even ex-spouses should be told first. Wouldn't your mother be crushed if she heard the news from your aunt's coworker's drycleaner?

## The Parents

**How do we decide which set of parents to tell first?** Traditionally the bride-to-be's family is told first. The groom's family is told next, and this should be done soon after.

**Once we are engaged, should our parents contact each other?** Traditionally, the groom's family contacts the bride's parents, either through a short note or phone call. Avoid e-mail, especially if this is their first contact. If the bride's parents are divorced, the groom's parents should call the parent who raised her and then call the other parent later. If the two families live close by, they can have brunch or drinks together and each can get an idea the other's expectations for the wedding. In some cases, it may be necessary for you and/or your fiancé to initiate this exchange.

 **Essential**

In today's world, it's unlikely that both sets of parents live in the same city or state as the bride and groom. Consider the possibility of using a webcam to announce the good news to everyone, at the same time, "in person." It's the next best thing to being there!

**What if my parents and fiancé have never met?** If you know the engagement is pending, as many do, try to bring your future husband home to spend a few days with your family before the engagement is official (or at least before sharing the news with everyone). Giving your parents and fiancé a chance to get to know each other before announcing your engagement starts you off on a solid foundation.

## The "New" Family

**My parents are divorced. Whom should I tell first?** You know your family better than anyone else. If you still live with a parent, they should be the first to know. Otherwise, whichever parent you are the closest to is told first. On the other hand, if you know your dad loves your fiancé and your mom doesn't, telling Dad first may be wise, as he may be able to help smooth it over with Mom.

**What if one of us has children?** If one of you has children, tell them right away. Don't risk them feeling excluded. They will want to know how a new mother or father will affect them. While it is not essential that children of a divorce give their consent, tremendous compassion should be used in breaking the news.

**How should I let my ex-spouse know I'm getting remarried?** A phone call would be fine. If you have children together, they should not be the ones to announce the news to your ex-spouse. Prepare for questions about alimony payments or custody arrangements. If you don't have kids, then your decision to tell your ex-spouse depends on your relationship with him.

## What's in a Name?

**How do I find out what my in-laws want me to call them?** If you are meeting your future in-laws for the first time, your fiancé should formally introduce you. This is the perfect moment to address this subject, as they will most likely tell you what to call them. Otherwise, simply ask. Chances are, if this is an issue for them, and sometimes it is, they will have said something directly to either you or your fiancé.

**What should my fiancé's children call me?** You want the children to call you something they feel comfortable with, and that may just be referring to you by your first name. If you have been a part of the children's lives throughout your dating relationship, the children have probably already decided what they are going to call you. If you are just coming into the children's lives, you will need to have a discussion with your fiancé about this; he may even need to speak with his ex-spouse.

## Announcing the Good News

After you've told family, it is time to share your joy with the world. No doubt the news will spread like wildfire at the sight of a ring on your finger. Before this happens, make an effort to personally contact your dearest friends and the special people in your life. On the other hand, it's okay to let the ring speak for itself with casual friends, business associates, and acquaintances.

**Should we announce our engagement in the newspaper?**
Publishing a formal announcement in the newspapers in your hometown and the city in which you work or currently live is a great way to spread the word and makes a great keepsake. Most newspapers have standard announcement formats to follow, which include names, education, and occupations of the bride, groom, and their parents and possibly a photograph. Check with your local paper for specifications.

 **Fact**

An engagement announcement for the newspaper typically reads as follows: Mr. and Mrs. (bride's parents) of (their city, state) announce the engagement of their daughter, (bride's first and middle name) to (groom's full name), son of Mr. and Mrs. (groom's parents' names) of (their city, state). A (month/season) wedding is planned. (Or, no date has been set for the wedding.)

**Does anyone still send out printed engagement announcements?** In the name of tradition, many couples do. A formal announcement printed from your stationer adds a level of formality to the wedding plans and provides a nice memento for years to come. Formal engagement announcements are traditionally sent by the parents of the bride, but can also be sent by the couple or the hosts of the wedding. They include basic information such as the hosts, who is marrying, and the location of the wedding. No date or times are mentioned.

## General Protocol

**Are the bride's parents the only ones who can make the engagement announcement?** The traditional protocol for mak-

ing an engagement announcement has the parents of the bri
to-be making the announcement of their daughter's engagemer
If the parents are divorced, then the mother makes the announce
ment, but the father must be mentioned. If a stepparent has raised
you, that parent may make the announcement with your mother
or father, but you should still mention the other parent. If both
parents are deceased, then a close relative does the honors. If the
couple is older and have been on their own, they may make the
announcement themselves.

## Let the Parties Begin!

Once all the major players have been notified, someone, usually
your parents, will throw a party in honor of you and your fiancé.
This party can be as formal or informal as the hosts would like.
The engagement party marks the official beginning of the wedding season.

### The Party

**When is the engagement party held?** The engagement party
should coincide with the publication of your announcement in
the newspapers, either at the same time or very soon after. If the
engagement will be short, the party should be held as soon as
possible so as not to interfere with any bridal showers or bachelorette parties.

**What is the most traditional way to have an engagement
party?** The parents or mother of the bride hosts a party at which
the formal announcement is made by the mother of the bride-
to-be, and the groom is presented to the friends and family. If
the bride lives in a different city from her parents, the party may
be held where she lives so that more of her friends can be in
attendance.

**n we have more than one engagement party?** The bride's
parents usually have first dibs on throwing the engagement party,
but the groom's parents or your friends may want to throw a party
too.

## Gifts

**Should I expect gifts at an engagement party?** Gifts aren't
required but are often presented, so beginning your registry is a
good idea. You should promptly send written thank-you notes for
any gifts you receive.

 **Alert**

Most stores that offer a Bridal Gift Registry will supply the
couple with small cards stating "Registered at . . . " It is not
acceptable to include these cards with your engagement
party invitation or your engagement announcement. Remember, announcing your engagement is not a license to ask for
gifts.

**Do I have to register for gifts?** A bridal registry is a service
that can only help you and your guests. While many couples hold
off on completing their registries until later (see Chapter 8), registering for some items now will provide guests with guidance
should they choose to purchase an engagement present. Most
department and specialty stores offer a free bridal registry service
and a staff consultant who will advise you on what items might be
useful for your new home.

# CHAPTER 2

# The Business of Being a Bride

*Y*ou thought planning a wedding was going to be fun. Well, it is fun, but it's also serious business. You are more than a bride. You are, in essence, the CEO of your wedding. You oversee vendors, crunch numbers, and keep friends and family happy and on task, all while organizing one of the most important days of your life. Approach your wedding planning with the same savvy you employ in life, and you will be right on track.

## Finding the Right Info

Weddings are a big business, and the amount of information out there can seem overwhelming. Taking some time to discover what wedding planning really entails will help you make informed decisions. Be sure to take advantage of anything that will help you gather information and educate yourself.

### What's Online?

**Can I plan my wedding on the Internet?** A large portion of your research and preplanning can be done with the Internet, but there are things you must do in person. There are numerous websites for all aspects of planning, from finding a dress to mapping out the honeymoon. In the case of wedding vendors, it cannot be stressed enough that you should always meet with a vendor in person before signing any contracts. You can also use the Internet to take advantage of the many bridal websites that are loaded

23

h planning tools, advice, real wedding stories, and paid vendor advertisements. Of course, there are tons of fabulous wedding products out there that you can order online. Truly, the Internet can cut out a lot of legwork and telephone calls, and most of the research can be done at your convenience.

 **Essential**

Bridal blogs are a unique way to gather "insider" info. Brides are not shy about their feelings, and you can learn from their planning triumphs and tribulations by reading their blogs. Just remember that this is one bride's personal view of wedding planning. Let the information guide you, but be sure to do your own homework too.

## Hitting the Streets

**I am thinking about attending a bridal show. Is it worth the effort?** It is definitely worth the effort. Once you are there, you have a great deal of information right at your fingertips. Seize the opportunity to meet vendors on the spot, see or taste samples of their work, and get a brief idea about their personality or style. From there, you can decide which vendors to meet with to discuss your wedding. If you go, wear comfortable shoes, bring your mom (or one friend), a sturdy bag to tote literature in, a camera, and a notepad.

**What is a wedding planning showroom?** At a wedding planning showroom (also referred to as a bridal showroom or a resource center), vendors display their work and products. You can come at your leisure with no obligation to view their work, gather information, and talk to the store personnel about your wedding plans. They are like super-convenient, year-round bridal shows with personal service.

## The Planning Path

You already have a life, right? You have a job, a family, and social obligations, but now you have a wedding to plan. Even if you are entertaining the idea of hiring a wedding planner, you still need to be organized and on top of the planning. There are simply too many items and issues that only you can take care of. Keeping the paperwork, swatches, and forms organized will help you keep your sanity from the beginning of the planning until your walk down the aisle.

## Staying Organized

**How do I stay organized and on top of my planning?** First, a filing system for hard copies of contracts and other forms should be established for your home and kept there for safekeeping. For your mobile planning, a three-ring binder with sheet protectors is the way to go. Make copies of contracts for the binder, place swatches and color chips in the pockets, and fill it up with tear-outs from magazines and other items that inspire you for your wedding. This system is easy to update and makes a perfect traveling companion.

## Staying on Track

**How do I know what I am supposed to do and when?** A comprehensive planning checklist will provide you with guidance and a general schedule of what needs to be done and when. Let the checklist keep you on track as you plan and nothing will slip through the cracks.

## Working with the Pros

Plan and plan, cross your "t's" and dot your "i's," but on the wedding day, your plans are in the hands of your vendors. The

...ationship you establish with your wedding vendors plays a major role in the success of the wedding day. If chosen wisely, vendors will be great allies. Research their qualifications and make sure you and the vendor have a good rapport and see eye to eye personality- and style-wise.

## Finding the One

**The ads in bridal magazines and on the web are so confusing. Everyone says they are "the best." How do I really know if a vendor is reliable and trustworthy?** These ads are placed by the vendors themselves, so of course they are going to be glowing endorsements. Search the Internet for reviews about the vendor. Unhappy brides tend to find a way to make themselves heard. Also ask each vendor for references, but keep in mind that vendors are not going to give you the phone numbers of people who are unhappy with their services. Finally, ask your wedding planner or your location manager for recommendations.

**The DJ we have selected is part of a large company that employs many different entertainers. How do I know who will be at my wedding?** You have to ask what the company's policy is, and you have to get a particular DJ's name on your contract to ensure that is who will be there on your wedding day. If the company is not willing to accommodate this request, decide if this variable is something you can live with. When you interview this company, always ask to meet with the person you would like to hire and see or hear samples of his work if applicable. If a vendor will be working closely with you on the wedding day, consider his personality too; you should actually like him if he is going to be with you all day. Entertainers and some photography studios, wedding planners, and videographers work this way.

**A vendor came highly recommended to me, but thus far I am not happy with his customer service. I want to hire him, but should I be concerned?** You should be concerned.

He may be very busy, which is understandable, but he should courting you for your business. If this is a service or product yo feel you cannot live without, you will have to make the decision about whether or not to try and work with him. If he is handling his business with you like this now when he presumably doesn't even have a contract or a deposit yet, do you really think it will get better once he gets paid?

 **Alert**

Once you have found the perfect vendor, it doesn't matter how friendly you are; this is still business! You must get a written contract that states the facts: dates, times, names, locations, cancellation policies, and payment schedules. Remember, it has to be signed by both parties.

## Vendor Etiquette

**We interviewed a number of photographers and have finally made a decision. Do I need to tell the ones we didn't choose that we will not be using them?** You have no obligation to tell a vendor you will not be using him. However, a quick e-mail, note, or phone call to let that vendor know you have chosen another is a courtesy. The vendor can then open up his schedule and cross you off his list. Some vendors are bold and may ask why you didn't select them or who you did select. You do not have to answer these questions if you do not feel comfortable doing so.

**I really love this photographer, but I know she is way out of my budget. My friend told me to meet with her anyway, because all vendors negotiate their prices. Is this true?** If you really like her work, call and talk to her first about your wedding date. Be truthful about your budget; otherwise you will be wasting the vendor's time as well as your own. Some vendors tweak their pricing for off-season weddings or for short notice

okings, but not all vendors negotiate their prices. It may be an
ption to have this photographer take engagement pictures or
other photos that may not be included in a typical wedding photography package.

 **Alert**

> To officially book a vendor for your wedding date, you need
> a contract. With the contract, expect to pay a nonrefundable
> deposit (usually 50 percent) at the time you book the vendor;
> the remaining balance will usually be due two weeks prior to
> the wedding date. Do not consider a vendor "yours" until you
> have a signed contract.

**My florist and I are not seeing eye to eye. Can a bride fire
a vendor?** Before you fire anyone, suggest to the florist you both
sit down and figure out what is going on. There was a reason
you hired her in the first place; let's see if you can get back to
that point and start fresh. If there is no hope for this, then parting
ways may be the best thing for both of you. But you must take
a couple of things into account: First, when is your wedding? Is
it far enough out that you will have time to find and work with
another florist? Secondly, you may not get your deposit back, so
you could end up being out some money. Additionally, depending on when the wedding date is, you may actually owe the florist
some money if she has already ordered flowers or supplies that
she cannot return. If this is still what you want, let the florist know
with a phone call and then follow up with a written confirmation.

**Do we need to feed the vendors at the wedding?** Many of
the vendors will be with you all day and you want them to be on
top of their game. A short break to have a meal and a beverage
really is not too much to ask. Some vendors even have this written into their contracts. Make arrangements with the caterer for

vendor meals, and provide the vendors with a table (far from guest tables) or a nearby room to eat their meal.

## Wedding Planners

You have heard the horror stories of wedding planners taking over and back-talking to the bride when she has an idea. But the truth is that the right wedding planner can be your greatest ally and friend. A wedding planner's purpose is to assist and guide the bride through the planning process, offering creative ideas and time-saving techniques and organizing all of the aspects of the wedding day. She is an invaluable asset to this special occasion.

### Working with a Planner

**My mother insists I have a wedding planner. I do NOT want one. How do I make her understand?** You should rejoice in the fact that your mother sees the value in a wedding planner and is presumably willing to pay for it. Wedding planners are quite helpful. As long as you have a say in who is hired, you could end up working with a wonderful planner on the details of your wedding. However, if you are dead set against it, make a list of your concerns and present them to your mother. Then interview a couple of planners and see if you still feel the same way. Feel free to present your concerns to the wedding planner, too.

**I have heard wedding planners make you use their vendors and that they get kickbacks or commissions from these vendors. I feel very uncomfortable with this. Is there anything I can do to avoid this situation?** What you have heard is somewhat true. Wedding planners typically prefer you to work with vendors they recommend or are familiar with. This is actually a benefit of working with a planner; she has relationships with vendors and knows what to expect from them. This will allow her to steer you away from vendors that do not fit your needs or budget. Some

…dors do offer kickbacks, or a percentage of the booking fee, …ck to the wedding planner when a client books them. However, …eputable businesses will not mark up their services in order to do this. If you really have an issue with this, you can flat out ask the vendor and the planner if this is a common practice for their business.

 **Essential**

> Imagine being a guest at your own wedding. A "day-of" wedding planner is a budget-friendly option that can make this a reality. While she doesn't work with you through the planning, she will take your carefully laid plans and work with the vendors, families, and wedding party on the wedding day to help make your wedding dreams come true.

### Benefits of a Wedding Planner

**I already have started planning. What can a wedding planner really do to help my planning?** A wedding planner can help you at any point. Some brides choose to hire a planner early on and have her involved from the earliest planning stages, including setting the date and selecting a venue. Even if you already have a good start on your planning, a wedding planner can review your work, refer you to vendors, make suggestions about décor and timing, and offer ideas about how to make this process run smoothly. A wedding planner is invaluable on the wedding day, acting as the point person for families, members of the wedding party, vendors, and guests. She will organize and execute the wedding plan, allowing you to enjoy your day.

## A Little Help, Please

As you go about your planning, don't forget you are not in this alone. Too many brides get caught up in the planning, start making decisions, and begin to feel that planning a wedding is chore rather than a wonderful experience. While there is muc to be done, delegating tasks will ease your workload, and allow others to contribute their talents and skills to your wedding. Call on your wedding party, your family, and most importantly your fiancé to help you plan this magnificent event.

## The Art of Delegating

**My father wants to be involved in the planning so badly. Any suggestions on how to do this?** Find a particular element of the wedding that he would be good at or interested in and see if you can find something for him to do. It will make him feel involved. For example, if he has a special interest in wine, ask him to be the man in charge of selecting wines for the cocktail hour and the various courses of dinner. If he is a car buff, he can help find your dream vehicle to drive off in on the wedding day.

 **Fact**

True, many grooms could do without getting involved in the nuts and bolts of planning, but there are plenty of tasks he can help you with, such as preparing his family's guest list, collecting addresses, and sampling cakes, the menu, and wine!

**My mother has a comment for every decision I make. How do I get my mother off my back while I am planning my wedding?** Your mother may be experiencing feelings of sadness and loneliness as she thinks about you getting married and moving on with your life. She may feel like she is losing you to your fiancé. Involve her in the planning to ease her fears. Ask her to accompany you while you gown shop or select flowers, or ask her to be in charge of selecting a choice of invitations for you to look at and approve. Chances are she just wants to spend some

ne with you. By making her a part of the planning, you will be
doing just that.

## Working with Friends

**I have already asked my longtime friends to be brides-
maids, but I have a handful of new friends that I would
love to include. Any ideas?** Ask the new friends to act as host-
esses on the wedding day, directing guests to their seats, providing necessary information, and assisting with the guestbook and
gifts. If any of them has a special talent, such as calligraphy, ask
if she will assist with invitations and place cards. You can also try
a favor-making party with these friends and they can assist you
in making favors and other small items you need for the wedding.

# CHAPTER 3

# Foundations of Planning

*O*nce you have acquainted yourself with the wonderful world of weddings, it is time to lay the foundation for your own wedding plans. These next few steps on the planning path are extremely important, as they will assist you with setting the tone for the event. It is finally time to pick that perfect date, find a wonderful location, hire vendors, and prepare the guest list. Oh, but you say this big to-do is not quite for you; well, consider getting away from it all with a destination wedding.

## The Big Day

The date you select for your wedding may hold some sentimental significance or may be a random pick, but whatever the choice, make sure you think through the variables of the date. In fact, you may want to select a season or month rather than a particular date to make your venue search a little easier. Along with selecting a date, you must decide on a time of day. These elements greatly influence the overall style, tone, and even budget for the wedding.

### The Date

**We really need to pick a wedding date. Where do we start?** In the preliminary search for a wedding date, select a season. Then look at your schedules and surroundings. Is a particular time of the year busy at work? Do your families always summer in Europe? Is summertime in your city just too hot to have an outdoor

s the winter weather simply too unpredictable in your
ese are all very real circumstances that can affect your deci-
nally, the venues you are looking at may already be booked
particular date, so you may need to be flexible if the venue
ice is more important than the actual date. Once you examine
e pros and cons of these factors, a date will fall into place.

**What are some factors we should consider when selecting a wedding date?** You should consider variables like holidays, religious celebrations, and community events. On a holiday week-end, your guests may encounter crowds and more expensive travel accommodations. During religious holidays, the house of worship may not be available, and some guests may be unable to attend. Finally, annual events that draw large crowds or require streets to be temporarily closed will also impact your plans.

**I just got engaged and really want to marry in the fall, but my sister is already getting married in the fall. Worse yet, the venue is only available two weeks before my sister's wedding. Should I go forward with my plans?** Is this fall wedding and venue so important you are willing to risk igniting a family feud? Chances are that unless your sister is the most under-standing, unselfish woman in the world, she will be less than pleased if you plan your wedding two weeks before hers. You really need to look at additional venue options that are available later in the fall, after your sister's wedding and honeymoon.

## Good Timing

**I want a formal wedding and would really love for it to be black tie, but my family church holds its last ceremony at 3:30 P.M. Is this too early for a black-tie event?** It is definitely too early for a black-tie designation. While you can still have a formal wedding, black tie should be reserved for weddings taking place in the evening.

**Fact**

The type of wedding you are dreaming of is affected by the time of day you select. Traditional guidelines for determining a wedding start time are: Brunch Reception, between 10:00 A.M. and 12:00 P.M.; Luncheon Wedding, between 12:00 P.M. and 2:00 P.M.; Tea Reception, between 2:00 P.M. and 4:00 P.M., Cocktail Reception, between 4:00 P.M. and 7:30 P.M.; Dinner Reception, between 5:00 P.M. and 7:00 P.M.

## Exploring Your Options

**I have always dreamed of an evening wedding, but are there any advantages to a daytime wedding?** There are advantages and disadvantages to all time slots. Daytime weddings can be just as magical as evening events; just select a style or theme that compliments the daytime hours, like a brunch or a tea. Daytime weddings can also have a positive impact on the budget; brunch and lunch usually cost less than dinner.

## The Guest List

The process (yes, it is a process) of compiling your guest list can be challenging, unless of course you have an open-ended budget and unlimited reception space. But if you're like most brides, you will need to make hard decisions when it comes to the guest list. Work with your fiancé and families to establish guidelines and create a guest list that suits your wedding plans.

## More Guests versus More Money

**My fiancé and I both come from large families with a tradition of big, fancy weddings. However, we have a limited budget and can't afford a dinner reception for 200 guests. What can we do?** There is no rule that states all weddings must in the evening and include an expensive sit-down meal. Even this is what your families usually do, you can break the mold and do something different. Opt for a morning or afternoon wedding and have a classy brunch or luncheon; your budget will go much further. Creativity and imagination are essential factors for a modern wedding. Most importantly, make the wedding fun and unique.

 **Essential**

> To cut costs, you may be tempted to invite some people to the ceremony but not the reception. Don't do it! It is like telling the guest, "We like you enough to invite you to the ceremony, but not enough to spend money on you at the reception." It is just plain tacky. The reverse, a smaller ceremony and a larger reception, is acceptable.

**Our guest list is larger than our venue and budget can accommodate. Is it okay to do a second invitation mailing if we receive many regrets the first time around?** It has become an accepted practice to have an "A" list and a "B" list when preparing the guest list. It's realistic to anticipate some regrets (on average, about 20 to 25 percent of invited guests will be unable to attend). This gives you the opportunity to send invitations to those people on your B-list. If you decide to do this, the first mailing should be sent a minimum of eight weeks before the wedding date; the second should be sent no later than five weeks prior. On a final note, be aware that the original reply date is already printed on the response card, so watch your mailing time.

## Sticky Situations

**My mother recently remarried and assumed that I would not be inviting my father to my wedding. It's important**

**to me that he is there, but my mother is threatening n to attend if my father does. What should I do?** You shoul feel free to invite anyone you choose to your wedding, regardless of family infighting. It is up to each invitee to accept or decline your invitation. If your mother refuses to attend, tell her that you're sorry and you will miss her. When she realizes you mean it, she may come around. Of course, budget factors may come into play if your mother is paying for the wedding, so you must be prepared for what could happen.

**My fiancé always seems to be on the verge of fisticuffs with his stepfather. Must we invite him to our wedding?** To invite your fiancé's mother without her husband would be awkward, rude, and offensive to his mother. If your fiancé insists on excluding his stepfather, he should discuss it first with his mother to find out the most tactful way to handle this.

If the situation is extreme, the stepfather will probably share your discomfort and choose not to attend.

## Guest Limitations

The easiest way to save some cash in the budget department is to cut the guest list. But how do you do that? Where do you draw the line? You really need to establish guidelines so that you can stay on point when creating this list.

**We have to cut people from our guest list. How do we decide who stays and who goes?** Establish guidelines and be consistent when creating the guest list. Make sure everyone agrees to and applies the rules across the board. The following are some policies to consider:

- **No children.** The fact that you're not inviting children is indicated to parents by the fact that their children's names do not appear anywhere on the invitation. Just to be safe, however, make sure your mother (and anyone else who might be questioned) is aware of your policy. What age you choose as a cut-off point between children and young adults is up to you.

- **No coworkers.** Unless you are counting on your wedding as a means to strengthen business ties, if you do need to cut somewhere, this may be a good way to go.
- **No distant relatives.** If you have a large immediate family, you may want to exclude distant relatives with whom you have no regular social interaction.

**Is it necessary to invite a guest's significant other?** You should always invite significant others of married guests, engaged guests, couples who live together, and those who are generally considered to be a couple. For those not in a committed relationship, it is a nice gesture but not necessary.

# The Perfect Place

It used to be easy. A ceremony was held at the family church, followed by a reception at the local hotel. That was then, this is now. Today, a marriage is a marriage, but a wedding is another thing entirely. Consequently, the choice of a wedding venue is one of the most important elements of your wedding. It sets the tone for the planning and plays a major role in all stylistic decisions.

## Selecting the Ceremony Venue

**How do I decide if we should marry in a house of worship?** First you need to examine your religious views and those of your fiancé. Then decide if marrying in a house of worship is the right thing to do for you as a couple. You may want to consult your parents; they will surely have an opinion about this matter. If you do not regularly attend a house of worship, you will need to find a location that will marry nonmembers.

**What are other options for a ceremony venue?** There are so many wonderful options for a ceremony. Public parks and gardens, the beach, a boat, the reception venue, city hall, and sometimes even your home are valid choices for holding a ceremony.

 **Alert**

> When you hold your ceremony in a public location, be prepared for onlookers. Everyone loves a wedding, and many will surely stand by to watch. If the idea of having strangers watch as you recite your vows makes you uneasy, look at more private options for this intimate moment.

**What else should I consider when selecting my ceremony location?** One of the most important aspects of selecting a ceremony site is its proximity to the reception venue. The two locations should be no more than a thirty-minute drive from each other. Additionally, you should also consider the accessibility of the site. For example, would you be crushed if your ninety-year-old grandmother couldn't make it down the rocky beachfront staircase to see you exchange vows? If so, you should really pick another location.

## Selecting the Reception Venue

**My dad thinks a wedding reception means cake and punch in the church's community room. How do I break it to him that times have changed?** The truth is cake and punch receptions are still done, and when it fits your lifestyle and budget it is a perfectly lovely option. But if this doesn't play into your ideal, you are going to need to provide your father with some facts about modern weddings. Show him some photos or even take him location hunting with you. It will be an eye-opener.

**The church has a ceremony time of 2:00 P.M. but we cannot begin the reception until 5:00 P.M. What do we do with our guests during this time?** Leaving your guests wondering what do for two hours is not considerate and may leave some guests with a complaint or two, but there are options. First, ask the reception venue manager if she has an area, like a garden or a meeting room, where you can have light refreshments set up during this time. You could make similar arrangements at a nearby restaurant. Another option is to ask a close friend or relative to have an "open house" during which time the guests can stop in for refreshments. Of course, the size of your wedding will determine if this is possible. Just remember these are your guests; keep them happy and entertained, and remember that they should not be paying for any of this.

## Other Considerations

**Does my location dictate the style of my wedding?** When you select your location, make sure it is complimentary to your wedding vision. Fighting against the established environment will give you nothing but trouble. Ultimately, the wedding could end up looking like a stylistic disaster, or it could cost you plenty of money to transform the location into your desired look.

**I am planning on getting married at a historic mansion. The rental fee is only $1,000. I should be able to save a lot of money, right?** Off-site locations have so many variables that additional expenses—valets, rentals, insurance, cleaning fees, security deposits, etc.—can add up quickly. While anything is possible, as a rule, off-site weddings typically cost more than weddings at traditional venues such as hotels, catering halls, and country clubs. You need to be a savvy budgeter to make this work. If possible, work with a wedding planner to pull this off without a hitch and within your budget.

**Fact**

Holding your ceremony and reception at the same location has its advantages: there is no travel time between venues; no transportation arrangements required for the guests, family or wedding party; less down time between ceremony and reception; and no need to worry about transporting flowers and other wedding paraphernalia to another site.

## Destination Weddings

Destination weddings started as a hot wedding trend, but they are now a staple in the wedding industry, making them a very viable option for the soon-to-wed. The location doesn't have to be exotic or sun-drenched to meet the requirements of a destination wedding. A grand castle in England, a ranch in Montana, or your hometown all fall into the category of a destination wedding if you have to travel to get to it.

### We're Leaving on a Jet Plane

**What are the advantages of holding a destination wedding versus a traditional wedding?** It is really hard to say that there is a distinct advantage to having a destination wedding. It is just different than a traditional wedding. It may be a more intimate wedding, because usually fewer guests can attend. It may also give you a sense of freedom to be away from your regular life, allowing you to concentrate on spending time with your family, your groom, and your guests. If you do plan a destination wedding, remember that you are the hosts for the three to four days the guests are there. You should plan activities, be a part of all the festivities, and provide travel and accommodation information.

**am afraid my guests won't be willing to travel or be able to afford it. How concerned about this should I be?** If you have been dreaming of a grand, 200-person affair for your wedding, then a destination wedding is probably not right for you. On average, expect a 50 percent attendance rate for a destination wedding, compared to the 75 percent plus for a traditional wedding. Economics and work schedules are a big factor in attendance. Another big consideration is the affordability of the destination.

## Planning Your Destination Wedding

**What are the steps for planning a destination wedding?** The following are the basic steps for planning a destination wedding:

- Hire a wedding planner or select an all-inclusive resort as your destination to guide you.
- Scout the site before booking.
- Inform the invitees of the travel arrangements and expenses via a Save-the-Date.
- Research the legalities for travel and marriage license requirements.
- Arrange accommodations for the guests at a local hotel.
- Plan a weekend full of activities, including transportation, and prepare an itinerary for the guests.
- Make arrangements for vendors traveling to the wedding.

**What are the challenges of planning a destination wedding?** Depending on your chosen locale, you may encounter difficulties that run the gamut from simple to complicated. Language barriers may make communicating with vendors and officials difficult. Be sure to arrange for a translator. Time differences may make it difficult to communicate with vendors or your planner, but e-mail may be your saving grace here. The availability of services or products that are "expected" at home may range from expensive to difficult to downright impossible to obtain.

**Alert**

One of the very first things you should do when planning your destination wedding is research the required travel documentation. It is also imperative to know the process for obtaining your marriage license and the identification you will need to get that all-important license.

**How and when do I let guests know we are having a destination wedding?** Let the guests know as soon as you have signed on the dotted line. Send Save-the-Dates nine to twelve months in advance (as opposed to six months for a traditional wedding), so that guests have time to schedule vacations and budget for travel expenses. Be sure to provide the guests with travel and accommodation information.

**Do we need to cover the guests' travel expenses?** You are not expected to cover the costs of the guests' airfare and hotel accommodations, but you may want to try to cover some costs for the wedding party. You are responsible for the reception costs, the cost of any planned activities, and transportation to and from the wedding and any activities. Of course, if you have the means, covering the travel expenses is fine.

## Returning Home

**Once we return home, is it okay to have a reception for those who could not attend?** A reception to celebrate your marriage is a great idea. You may include those who could not attend the wedding as well as those who were there. Plan to display photos and possibly play the wedding video so that all the guests can enjoy your memories.

 **Essential**

At your post-wedding celebration, feel free to wear your wedding dress and include traditional activities such as a cake cutting and a toast. However, remember that gifts are not obligatory for this type of party, although many guests may bring them anyway.

**Do we send invitations for the reception?** Definitely send invitations. They do not need to be as formal as a wedding invitation, and remember to word the invitation properly. Since you are already married, this is a celebration, not a wedding.

## Who Needs Guests?

You're the kind of girl who hasn't been dreaming of her wedding since she was five. Maybe you are not interested in being the center of attention. Maybe you cannot imagine spending oodles of cash on one day. Maybe there are family dynamics that you just do not want to deal with on your wedding day. Well, eloping may be just what the doctor ordered.

**The more we think about it, we are really not into the idea of a big wedding. Can we just run off and get married?** Yes! An elopement is just the two of you heading off to get married and surprising everyone when you return. You don't have to run far to elope, either. You can easily get married by a justice of the peace or at the courthouse where you obtain your marriage license. Some couples just hire an officiant to meet up with them at the local beach or park to perform a low-key ceremony. You will have to check into the local marriage license requirements to see if there is a waiting period or if you will need witnesses. When you make the big announcement, be prepared for shock, delight, and possibly some dismay from those, like your parents, who were wishing for the big wedding.

**If we elope, can we have a reception to celebrate with friends?** A reception to celebrate with your friends is totally acceptable, and it's a great way to celebrate. Some couples have elected to surprise their guests by inviting them to a party and then making the big announcement. The more traditional route is to include the reception invitation with the wedding announcements so that the guests know why they are attending a party.

# CHAPTER 4

# Money Matters

*Y*our parents are nervous, your in-laws are in a panic, and you just don't know where to begin! Until you have a frank discussion about money, the wedding budget is the proverbial elephant in the room. No matter whether you have six figures or $6,000 to spend, a wedding is a large investment. While talking money is not the "fun" part of the wedding, it is necessary.

## Crunching the Numbers

Too often couples sit down to sort out the wedding budget with no sense of what a wedding costs or what it takes to get them from A to Z. They have grand ideas but no concept of how those ideas translate into reality or how much those ideas really cost. The amount of cash it will take to pull off the wedding of your dreams is all too often greeted with astonishment.

### Wedding Costs

**Are there any guidelines to help me figure out how much I should spend?** It is hard to make a blanket statement about what weddings cost. Two of the largest factors are the size and location of the wedding. For example, a big wedding in New York City will set you back more than a big wedding in Little Rock. The date you select will also affect your final costs. May through September are considered prime or high-season wedding dates.

Maybe one of the biggest factors in determining how much a wedding will cost is your own personal taste. If you have grown up eating caviar at the finest restaurants, a cake and punch reception at the local community center is probably not going to satisfy you, although it might work for someone else. To get a basic idea of the cost of a wedding in your area, ask recently married friends and check out local wedding websites (many vendors post prices). Scheduling a budget consultation with a wedding planner is an invaluable resource. Many planners will charge an hourly fee, and you can pick their brains for budget information.

 Fact

The single biggest wedding expense you will incur is your reception. As a rule, expect half of your total budget to go toward those costs, which include the menu and the venue. The remainder of the budget is divided among the other wedding costs. Prioritize the remaining components and budget accordingly.

**My fiancé and I have saved about $10,000 over the last few years. We do not expect our parents to contribute to the budget. Is it possible to pull off a wedding for $10,000?** Anything is possible, but you have to be realistic. $10,000 will not get you into the most sought-after hotel in town, or allow you to invite 200 guests to a sit-down black-tie dinner. The key is to make the money you have work for you. As you will hear time and again, the best way to make your money go further is by limiting the guest list. Additionally, be wise when you select a venue and a time. Consider a morning or afternoon wedding, when you can offer a lighter menu.

## Finding the Cash

**We are considering charging the bulk of our wedding expenses on a credit card. We'll earn rewards and can easily finance our wedding this way. Is this a good idea?** As long as you have the funds to pay the bills when they come in, charging wedding expenses on a credit card is a fine idea, especially if you are earning airline miles or other rewards. Keep in mind that many credit cards have high interest rates and you will pay a lot of money in interest if you wait to pay off your bills.

 **Alert**

While it may seem like the most important thing in the world at this moment, cashing out a 401(k) or an investment account or taking a second mortgage out on your home to finance your wedding is a bad idea that can jeopardize your future financial security.

## Who Pays for What?

Once upon a time the bride's parents were expected to host the wedding. However, times have changed, and many parents of the bride are thankful for that. Taking a closer look at traditional wedding expenses will give you an understanding of what goes into paying for a wedding and maybe some idea on how to lighten the load for your parents.

### Traditional Wedding Expenses

**What is the traditional breakdown of wedding expenses?**

**The bride and her family usually pay for:**
- Bride's dress and accessories
- Invitations, reception cards, and announcements

- Fee for the ceremony site
- Flowers for the ceremony and reception
- Attendants' bouquets
- Bride's father's and grandfather's boutonnières
- Music for the ceremony and reception
- Groom's wedding ring and gift
- Photography and videography
- Housing and gifts for the bridesmaids
- Limousines/transportation
- Reception costs (venue, food, liquor, and décor)

**The groom and his family traditionally pay for:**
- Bride's wedding and engagement rings
- Bride's bouquet and gift
- Marriage license
- Officiant's fee
- Corsages for the mothers and grandmothers
- Boutonnières for the groom, groomsmen, his father, and grandfather
- Ushers' and groomsmen's housing and gifts
- Rehearsal dinner
- Honeymoon

**The bride's attendants usually pay for:**
- Their dresses and accessories
- A shower gift
- Bridal shower
- Bachelorette party
- Their own travel expenses
- Gift for the couple

**The groom's attendants usually pay for:**
- Their tuxedoes or suits
- Bachelor party
- Their own travel expenses
- Gift for the couple

## Money Talks

**My parents are paying for the wedding. Does that mean I don't get a say in the planning?** Parents often feel they should have some say when they are handing over cash, but no matter who's paying for the wedding, you and your fiancé are the only people who should ultimately decide what your wedding will be like. When working with reasonable parents, you should be able to accept their financial help and at least consider their wishes and concerns.

 **Fact**

Diligence and self-control are required to prevent you from going overboard and over budget. You can and should provide a safety net for yourself. Factor in a percentage of the budget, 10 percent for example, for last-minute or unexpected expenses. There are always some.

**If my fiancé's parents want to invite a lot more people than mine, shouldn't they offer to cover the extra cost?** The families of the bride and groom should try to have a balanced guest list. But if your future father-in-law insists on inviting all of his great-aunts and second and third cousins, your fiancé should speak with his parents about contributing some money to defray costs.

## Creative Financing

After all this talk of who is supposed to pay for what, it comes time to figure out how your wedding is really going to be paid for. While the bride's parents traditionally finance a major portion of the wedding, it is common for the groom's parents to contribute to the budget. Often, because couples are marrying later in life and have the financial means to do so, the bride and groom also finance a portion or sometimes the entire wedding themselves. To sum it up, it really doesn't matter where the money comes from anymore.

## Divvying Up the Expenses

**Can I ask my fiancé's parents to pay for part of the wedding?** Talk to you parents first, and if it is important to them to be the hosts of the wedding, try to respect their wishes and keep your wedding on a scale that is within your family's budget. If you or your fiancé want something more elaborate than your parents can realistically afford, you should accept that financial responsibility. If you really feel the need to ask his parents for money, you should discuss it with your parents first, and then your fiancé (not you) should talk to his parents about contributing.

**To help offset expenses can we have a cash bar at the reception?** Cash bars have traditionally been considered taboo; however, they are steadily becoming more commonplace. Strictly speaking, your guests should come to your wedding without having to pay for their own drinks (or anything else). If budget is a concern, offer a soft bar (beer, wine, and soft drinks), and forego premium alcohol.

**I just found out that my church is playing host to another wedding ceremony on the same day as mine. Would it be okay for me to ask whether the other couple wants to use the same flowers and split the cost?** It doesn't hurt to ask, as long as you are not planning to reuse these flowers at your reception. Of course, the other couple may decline the offer, and then you will need to make other plans.

## Quick Cash Savers

There really are so many ways to save money and stay within your budget without offending or upsetting anyone, or sacrificing your vision of wedding style. With a little research and imagination, you can discover creative solutions and alternatives to the most common bridal budget dilemmas.

## What to Cut

**Is it necessary to give favors to guests?** Favors aren't required, and some couples choose to forego this tradition completely. If you would like to provide the guests with a memento of your wedding, keep in mind that favors need not be expensive. Ideas for inexpensive favors include small boxes of chocolate, candy-coated almonds, or packets of seeds for flowers.

## Best Ways to Save

**Can we really save money through heavy-duty negotiating or even sponsorship of our wedding?** Talented and respectable vendors may offer slight discounts for off nights like Thursday and even Friday, last-minute bookings, and weddings in off-season months like January, but for the most part you are not going to be able to talk them into shaving thousands of dollars off their price. Some vendors are willing to negotiate (to an extent), and some may be willing to exchange items or services—for example, swapping a large framed engagement photo for some extra pages in your wedding album. As for sponsorship, it is probably the tackiest idea ever.

**How can we save money without making an etiquette faux pas?**
- Have fewer attendants. This means fewer bouquets, boutonnières, and thank-you gifts.
- Consider a weekday, Friday evening, or Sunday wedding to defray costs. Saturday is the most popular and, therefore, most expensive day to get married.

- Don't plan for a mealtime reception. An afternoon event between lunch and dinner times or an adult cocktail party (after dinner) is a great option, and you can offer hors d'oeuvres and cake rather than a full meal.
- Have a friend ordained or deputized to marry you.
- Consider décor options other than floral arrangements. Use lanterns and candles (if they are allowed), seashells, or potted plants.
- Skip the champagne and have the guests toast with whatever they are drinking.
- Trim one hour off the reception time. Many venues book weddings in five-hour time blocks, but depending on your event, three to four hours may be plenty of time. You will save on drinks and musician/DJ time.
- Downsize the wedding cake and order a sheet cake to be cut and served from the back.

## Contracts

This is your wedding, but it is also a business. As you plan your wedding, you will be faced with numerous decisions, among them selecting a wedding venue and hiring wedding professionals. You will expect a certain level of service. They will also have expectations of you. To ensure wedding-day success, be sure to have detailed contracts with each wedding professional.

### Get It in Writing

**I found this great florist, but she says she doesn't do contracts. I really want to work with her, but feel a bit uneasy about the situation. What should I do?** Wedding professionals should offer written contracts. They not only protect the bride, but they also protect the vendor. You might want to consider finding another florist, but if this is not an option, ask her if she is agreeable to you writing out the details of the agreement and both of you signing it.

**When I called my DJ yesterday he said he never received my signed contract and booked my wedding date with another client. I just had not gotten around to mailing the contract back. Can he do that?** If you never returned the signed contract and deposit, he probably just assumed you changed your mind. Mind you, he should have called or e-mailed you to check on your status. Officially you never booked him, and he was free to move on. Be sure to always return paperwork and payments on time. Always look on the contract for an expiration date on the contract as well.

**I have made many changes with my caterer since signing the contract. He says "okay" to everything. Is it really okay?** The caterer should update your file and send you updated written confirmations as you go. Be sure the changes reflect the details and the prices you discussed.

 **Essential**

Wedding insurance protects your wedding investment. In the grand scheme of things, wedding insurance is relatively inexpensive, but most important, it provides protection against such things as cancellations, damages, personal and liquor liability, and vendor no-shows.

**Are there any precautions I can take when I sign the contracts?** Be sure all of the details are included. Don't let the florist write "five bridesmaids' bouquets" on the contract. Have them specify the types of flowers to be used and every detail down to the color of the ribbon. Just keep everything detailed.

# Hey, Big Tipper

Brides and grooms often overlook one very substantial expense—tips! Depending upon the size of your reception, tipping can easily add a few hundred to a few thousand extra dollars to your costs. Some wedding professionals include a gratuity in their contract and then expect an additional tip at the reception. As a result, whom to tip and how much can often be a perplexing dilemma.

## Why Tip?

**I just don't get it. I have already paid these vendors a lot of money. Do I really need to tip them?** Some vendors expect a tip and even make mention of it in their contract or in face-to-face meetings, but it is not mandatory. Tipping is and should continue to be a reward for extraordinary service.

**At my friend's wedding, the caterer was horrible, but she still had to tip them. Should she have skipped the tip?** There is a difference between the catering company and the servers and workers who were at the wedding. Chances are those tips went to the service staff and bartenders who, hopefully, earned it. Sometimes when a vendor's service is questionable you need to look at the bigger picture to see who the tip will benefit and who is really responsible.

## Tipping Guidelines

**How much should we tip?** Exactly how much or whom you tip is completely at your discretion. The scale of your wedding, your wedding venue, and your geographical location will influence final tipping amounts. The following are simply guidelines, not rules. Many of the guidelines offer percentages, but flat fees are acceptable, no matter what the amount. On a final note, if you cannot afford to tip everyone, a glowing thank you card is always appreciated.

- Caterers and reception site managers usually have gratuities of 15 percent to 20 percent included in their contracts, which are usually paid in advance by the host of the reception. If the caterer or manager has been exceptionally helpful, you may wish to give her an additional tip, usually $1 to $2 per guest.
- The banquet captain runs the venue's portion of the reception. He oversees all of the food and beverage service, and sees that the guests are comfortable and happy. He should be tipped approximately $1 to $5 per guest depending on the location.
- Wait staff usually receive 15 percent to 20 percent of the food bill or $10 to $20 per server. Caterers sometimes include this gratuity in their contract. If the tip was not paid to the caterer in advance, give the tip to the headwaiter, maitre d', or banquet captain during the reception.
- A wedding planner is paid a fee for her service, but if your planner has provided you with exceptional service and care during the planning and on the wedding day, a tip is in order. Ten percent of her fee or anywhere from $50 to $500 is acceptable.
- Bartenders should be tipped in the range of $50 to $100. The location and size of your wedding should determine the amount. For example, a bartender for a small wedding at a moderately priced restaurant would fall into the $50 range, while a bartender at a wedding for two hundred guests at an expensive hotel should be tipped more in the $100 range.
- Restroom, coat check, or parking attendants should be prepaid by the host, usually $1 to $2 per guest or car. Ask the staff not to accept tips from guests.
- Limousine drivers receive 15 percent to 20 percent of the bill. This tip is almost always included in the contract. Any additional tips are at the host's discretion.

- Musicians or DJs may be tipped if their performance was exceptional. Tips usually run about $25 or more per musician. DJs are tipped in the range of $50 to $200.
- Florists and bakers are not usually tipped; you simply pay a flat fee for their services. If you do choose to tip, 15 percent is standard.
- Photographers and videographers are not usually tipped; you simply pay a flat fee for their services. If the vendor works for a studio, you can tip $50 to $250. This amount would depend on how pleased you are with the service provided by the photographer and the overall scale (budget) of your wedding.
- Delivery personnel or setup staff receive $5 to $20 each.
- Makeup artists and hair stylists should be tipped 15 percent to 20 percent of their bill.
- A hired officiant receives a flat fee for performing the service. A tip of $50 to $200 could be in order if the service was exceptional. The actual amount would depend on the length and details of the ceremony, as well as the amount of time and care the officiant spent with you prior to the wedding. For example, an officiant who meets with you for premarital counseling and helps you to personalize your ceremony should be tipped more than an officiant that simply shows up and "reads straight from a book." A religious officiant usually asks for a donation to his house of worship. This ranges from $50 to $500. This amount is typically outlined when you book the house of worship, or you may ask the officiant or venue coordinator for customary amounts. A civil officiant, like a judge, is not allowed to accept tips.

**Is it okay to tip after the wedding?** A tip is always a welcome surprise, and tipping after the wedding is fine. Send a thank-you note along with the tip. The vendor will be thrilled. If you really cannot tip, a glowing letter of recommendation and the offer to be a reference is always appreciated.

# CHAPTER 5

# Social Media and Your Wedding

*I*t is hard to deny that social media has permeated modern life. Everywhere you look, everywhere you go . . . social media is there. There are Facebook pages and Twitter handles, not to mention Pinterest, Flickr, and simply everyone has a blog! And that is just the tip of the iceberg. Some couples are ready to take their wedding to the next level—sharing it all on social media. Other couples are looking to put what they already know to good use when planning, and then there are some who just cannot imagine the thought of anyone tweeting about their plans. Finding a way to manage the pros and cons of social media is a major part of the *new* wedding experience.

## The Who, What, and Where of Social Media

How will social media factor into your wedding plans? Will you use it to communicate with guests? Find vendors? Or do you want to trend on Twitter? Just ten years ago e-mail and wedding websites were about the extent of social media any bride or groom utilized to plan their weddings. Since then, the reach of social media has grown by leaps and bounds. Social media has afforded couples many, many advantages, but it also has its pitfalls. There are numerous ways to make social media work for you and your wedding . . . you just need to sort them all out.

## Psst . . . Pass It On

**Why should I consider using social media in my wedding planning?** Disseminating information is one of the key components of social media. You may not want everyone in the city or state or world for that matter (you never know what will go viral) to see photos of your bridal shower or know where and when you are honeymooning, but being able to communicate almost instantly with a vendor when you have a question, or research how to make those cute favors is quite useful.

 **Essential**

Be sure to check the privacy settings on all of your accounts regularly. Even if they are set to private or "friends only" sometimes system upgrades on social media sites reset your personal settings.

**How can I share and update information with the wedding party, family, and vendors using social media?** There are many ways to use social media to ease your planning and pass information along to the friends, family, wedding party members, and vendors, for example:

- **Facebook:** Facebook has been around since 2004 and its impact and reach increases daily. As of June 2012, Facebook reports there are 955 million monthly active users. What may have started as a simple tool for (young) adults to interact has become a daily staple for people of all ages. Heck, your grandma may even have a page! You can not only "friend" your best friend from the second grade, but you can "like" company pages to keep updated on deals, promotions, and new ideas.
- **Twitter:** How much can you say in 140 characters or fewer? It may surprise you at the amount of information that flows

through Twitter as well as the relationships that are forged with those 140 characters. Users send over 150 million tweets every day. Twitter happens in real time . . . it moves fast. You can follow wedding taste-makers and style gurus, and you can create lists with particular tweeters based on what you are looking for.

- **Blogs:** Blogs are hugely popular, and attract much attention from social media and conventional media. Blogs are ever-changing, and blogging is a great way to interact with others and document certain aspects of your planning and preparation. You may not want to post photos of yourself trying on your gown, but you may want to share a few photos of the venue or a crafty creation. You can update a blog daily (or more often).
- **Websites:** Brides and grooms have been using wedding websites for a while now. Many companies offer free wedding websites and some charge a fee; it really depends on the sophistication of the website you want. If you are tech savvy, you can even create and host your own. Websites are different from blogs because while you can update them, they are more static, meaning particular information remains constant. Couples use websites for detailed, pertinent information regarding accommodations, directions/maps, registry links, and may even take RSVPs through their sites.
- **Newsletters:** Using a company like Mail Chimp affords you the ability to send out newsletters to your guests with updates on accommodation information, directions to events, changes in scheduling, and other important notices. It is easy to create a simple newsletter and send it off to your guests letting them know of changes or updates.

## Pretty Pictures

**There are so many gorgeous ideas online. Is there a good way to keep track of all these ideas?** At one time, brides carried their cameras around with them, snapping photos at the florist, at the dressmaker, at the venue. Now things have been streamlined. With your smartphone, iPhone, or tablet you can snap photos of all things wedding and nonwedding that inspire you or that you want to remember . . . and then you can share those ideas if you choose to. There are quite a few ways to catalog the gorgeous images and ideas you find online too. Look at these very cool tools that can help:

- **Pinterest:** Pinterest is a virtual online bulletin board. You create boards (flowers, candles, gowns, favors, etc.) and as you scan the Internet or Pinterest itself you "pin" the image with the correct URL/web address that corresponds to it. When you are ready to revisit that particular element, you know where to find it. Pinterest has only been around since 2010, but its impact is huge and the number of users grows each day.

- **Flickr:** Flickr allows you to upload photos from just about any digital or mobile device or photo application to its service. Once uploaded, your photos are open for comments and conversation back and forth with other users. Should you decide to, you can easily share these photos via other social media sites as well.

- **Instagram:** Snap a photo, create some cool effects and then post it to your Twitter, Facebook, Flickr, Tumblr, and Foursquare. These photos are shared with your followers and others. It is not only a fun and popular app for your phone, but a very cool way to instantly keep track of things you love and ideas that pique your interest, and just have a little photographic fun!

 **Fact**

You should be careful what you say and post on social media. It can be shared and manipulated by hackers, thieves, frenemies, and unseemly characters. Good rule of thumb—don't post anything online you wouldn't want your mom to know!

## We're on the Air

**My dearest friend will be overseas when I get married. Additionally there are some other family members who cannot travel. What is the best way to share the day with them?** With today's technology everyone can attend your wedding . . . sort of. Some guests may be unable to travel for health or other myriad reasons, but they can still get a peek at your nuptials! Once upon a time you would buy DVDs or copies of photos and send them to guests who could not attend your wedding. Now, a live streaming feed of your wedding is the way to share with those who cannot attend. You can DIY it (with your Internet connection, a service, and a camera) or you can hire a company that can come in with a professional videographer and set it all up.

# Social Media Strategy

Social media can facilitate your wedding planning. On your lunch hour you can scan Pinterest for great ideas, you can send off a few e-mails to vendors, and maybe even tweet a couple of companies with questions. The ease and reach of social media is vast and can certainly make life easy, as well as cut down on hours spent doing research. It is absolutely true that, in certain respects, social media has streamlined life and made a wealth of knowledge accessible at a moment's notice.

## How It Can Help

**I am very traditional, and more importantly, so are my parents. Is using social media for my wedding an etiquette faux pas?** Before you decide for or against using social media to help you plan your wedding, you must take a look at what it can do for you. When utilized correctly, social media is a great tool, but when not used correctly—when used without a "social filter"—social media can be hurtful and overwhelming too. Here are some of the ways it can help you:

- You can connect with wedding suppliers and wedding vendors via social media. "Liking" a company's Facebook page or following a Twitter feed or a blog may give you access to additional discounts, daily deals, insights as to how the vendors work, and almost instant access to them, as well as a glimpse into what others are saying about them online.

- You can pass along information quickly and easily. This not only applies to your vendors and suppliers but to your invited guests and wedding party as well. Just think about how many people you know that are alerted every time they receive a text, e-mail, or a message/posting on social media. It's instant access!

- You can create a group for invited guests (or the wedding party, etc.) on Facebook. If you are going to use groups to disseminate information through social media, you need to make sure the group is private so that not everyone can access it. You cannot assume that everyone wants to hear about the wedding, especially if they are not invited. You can also set up a private blog to share information.

- There is no shortage of amazing inspiration and décor on the web. Sites like Pinterest allow you to have your own virtual bulletin board where you can gather ideas and save them for future reference.

- You can help far away family members feel like they are a part of the planning. Maybe your mom lives out of town, maybe your sister has always imagined being by your side but she just can't be there. Share details about your planning by using social media tools like Flickr or a smaller private group page on Facebook. You can snap and share photos, upload images, and share all the other details as you plan to help make distant relatives feel like they are included.

# ❓ Question

How do I decide which social media tools to use when planning my wedding?
Chances are you are already familiar with many social media channels. If so, use the ones you prefer and that most of your friends and family have access to for planning and sharing information. You may find you want to add one or two additional programs to compliment what you already know.

## How Social Media Can Hurt

**How could anyone be bothered by my sharing the details about the wedding via social media? Aren't they happy for me?** For all the good social media can do, it can be come too much . . . *you* can become too much on your social media outlets. Weddings are fun and fabulous and your best friend and mom may want to know every detail, but that does not mean all of your friends and connections do. Brides tend to overshare and with the ease social media provides, oversharing is quite the issue. Here are some ways to avoid using social media:

- You may want to post your engagement on Facebook. You might want to share all of the details of your event. In fact, a countdown to the big day sounds divine, but hold it right there. Unless every single one of your "friends" is invited there will be some hurt feelings. Even though these "friends" may be happy for you, seeing and hearing about all the amazing things happening in your life when they are not included can hurt.
- Even for those who are invited and a part of the festivities, if you post wedding updates every hour, they are going to get tired of it really quickly. There *can* be too much of a good thing. If you become obsessed and single minded with your wedding planning people are going to tune you out.

- Being obsessed with anything is not pretty. Brides tend to be an obsessive group anyway and with the mobile devices available now, a bride can take obsession to new levels. Spending your days with your eyes glued to a screen, scrolling through wedding ideas, tweeting vendors, liking Facebook pages, and uploading photos to Instagram and Flickr, well, let's just say your fiancé may not even want to be near you.

 **Alert**

If you share every last detail of your wedding on social media channels, what are you leaving the guests to be wowed with on the wedding day? Show or share too much of your wedding plans and you may end up with unsolicited advice before the big day and really miss that wow factor with your guests on the wedding day.

## Time for a Status Update

A ring. A magical question. A need to tell everyone! Easy, right? Just grab your mobile device, snap a photo, and let the world know you are engaged . . . right? WRONG! It may be tempting to announce the news to almost everyone with a few clicks, but that is not the right way to do it. Read on to find out how to gracefully use social media to plan and communicate.

### The Right Way

**Can I just send a big social media blast to everyone to tell them the news of the engagement?** You may be one half of a modern tweeting, texting, sharing couple, but that does not mean all of your guests are. Or, even if they are, seeing a status update or getting an e-mail may not be the way they want to hear the news of an engagement. With so many options, how do you make it all work? No matter what the inner social media maven inside you says, you must use the telephone if not a face-to-face meeting to tell those closest to you that you are engaged. Your parents, then your fiancé's parents, especially need to be told before you tell the world. But don't stop there. Be sure to tell other close friends and relatives the news before you post it online.

**When is it okay to announce our engagement via social media?** There is really no official time frame or waiting period before you post any updates on your marital status. Some say two weeks, some say never. Most importantly, you need to make sure that those closest to you have been told in person or via telephone (yup, the old-fashioned way!). After that, whether or not you announce your engagement on social media is up to you, but do it subtlety and tastefully. And if you do, be warned there will be those who, after following the news of your planning, will be hurt when they never receive an invitation.

**Can I post a photo of my ring on Facebook?** Again, you must make sure that all of those important people in your life know the news first. Posting a photo of the ring on social media can seem ostentatious, so be careful when you do this. Perhaps a single shot of the two of you with the ring showing is a better idea than creating an album with seventy-five different angles of the ring.

## Use It!

**It is so easy to communicate with people via social media. I plan on using it to its fullest extent. What is a good way to do this?** On Twitter you can create a list that includes all of those invited to the wedding, but realize your Twitter feed is still public. If you feel the need to tweet, consider setting up a wedding Twitter account with protected tweets, meaning those friends and family members who know about it need to be approved (by you) to follow you.

 **Essential**

The most subtle way to announce your engagement on Facebook or any other social media site with marital status as an option is to simply change that status on your profile page to engaged. It is simple, "quiet," and won't leave anyone thinking you are just showing off.

**I am on Facebook all the time and so are all of my friends. Why can't I just post everything there?** No one is stopping you, but hopefully your better judgment will. Consider setting up a private group on Facebook. You can create a private page and invite only those who are invited to the wedding. Then you have a private forum to share away and post wedding updates. Anyone who accepts the invitation for the page should be fully aware of what it is for. You can also create multiple groups to accommodate different needs, for example, one for wedding party, and for your mother, sister, and maid of honor. Just be sure not to make a lot of announcements on your public page telling everyone to "head over to the (private) wedding page to see the latest news." That kind of defeats the purpose.

## The Wrong Way

**We just registered! I am so excited to let everyone know what we want. Can I post the link to the online registry on social media?** As social media etiquette is just coming into play, you can actually get away with a lot of things as everyone learns what the rules are, but posting a gift-giving link on any social media site might seem a little greedy. Such links are best left to the wedding website where people expect them to be. If someone asks you this question directly (even if it is in a public forum, like on your Facebook wall), send him or her a private message with the information.

**I have so much to share. I am excited to share my wedding planning experience with everyone? Do I need to limit my posts?** Too much wedding chatter anywhere, even in real life, will turn people off. That does not mean they are not happy for you, but the rest of the world is living a regular life, and probably does not want to be inundated with wedding chatter all day long. Keep control and try to post updates on your private wedding group pages. Also, space your posts out, and don't forget to add in some other nonwedding updates too. Be sure to interact with people on other topics besides your wedding.

 **Essential**

Wedding planning can be hard work. Dealing with logistics and money and family can take its toll, but keep the negativity off of social media channels. Dealing with frustrations and airing dirty laundry are best left offline.

## Guest Considerations

There are a lot of ways to make social media work in your wedding plans, but you need to remember that not all guests are social media pros. Grandma may not be into checking a blog or Facebook. For that matter your parents may not choose to access these tools either. You need to find ways to use social media, but not exclude those who do not use it.

### Oh No, You Didn't!

**Can I just e-mail the invitation to everyone?** Even for the most casual weddings, e-mailing an invitation would not be considered proper. For a formal wedding this would confuse the guests, as the invitation should match the tone and style of the event. But even for a casual affair, an e-mail is way too impersonal and much too informal of a way to invite the people you are closest with to your wedding.

**A very distant friend continues to post somewhat negative things about me and my wedding on social media. Can I make her stop?** If you have not already, contacting this friend is the first thing to do. Explain the situation and ask her to please stop this behavior. She may think she is being funny . . . even if you, or no one else, is not getting the joke. Chances are she just may be immature enough to think that this is a good way to lash out for not being invited. Most social media avenues have ways to block or moderate comments from particular users, which can prevent them from being able to post anything on "your space." If the behavior continues, you can also report her to whichever platform she is posting the offensive behavior on.

## Info to Go

**In an effort to be green and easily communicate with my guests, I want to send information via e-mail or newsletter. Is this tacky?** How you use social media is what determines if it is tacky or not. Blasts of information such as "Engagement party is in two days. Don't forget we are registered at . . ." is tacky. Anything that announces major invite-only events to masses of people who are not invited or is a post disguised as a "don't forget to bring a gift" statement is in bad taste. Using social media to privately communicate with only those who are invited is perfectly acceptable. Private groups and e-mailed newsletters in conjunction to your blog or website is how information can and should be conveyed.

 **Fact**

Set up a private group or invitation-only blog for invitees that allows you to post necessary and relevant information and answer questions for those who need to know. When you do this, be sure not to announce it on a public forum. Saying "Hey, all of you who are invited to the wedding (private) group, there is a new message up," is not a good idea.

**Quite a few of my guests are not on social media. How do I get the information to them?** Even if you are utilizing social media to disseminate information quickly, you still need to provide certain information in printed/mailed form. Until the day comes (and it surely will) when everyone is connected to social media somehow, passing on information such as accommodations, travel, attractions, and directions will need to be done "the old fashioned way."

## Social Media Versus the Bride

Unless you are the royal couple and can request (require) that everyone turns off their phones as they arrive at the wedding, you are going to need to contend with social media at your wedding. There is a time and place for it, if you want it there. Someone is going to take a photo and share it online. Someone will tweet. You just need to decide if you want to encourage it. If you do, here are some ideas:

### Acceptable Behavior

**When is it acceptable to use social media at a wedding?** There is not one set answer to this question. Really it depends on the couple and their take on wedding traditions. Most experts agree that texting and tweeting during a ceremony should be off limits. No guest should stand up mid-ceremony to get a better photo so they can Instagram it. It is just common sense. However common sense seems to be disappearing quickly. If the guests are involved in social media interactions when they should be attentive and part of the larger event, it is considered rude. However, if you are trying to trend on Twitter, you will want the guests to be tweeting at any and all other convenient times. Making social media a part of your wedding can be fun, but it can also be a distraction.

## Head Tweeter

**It is a dream of mine to trend on Twitter. Since I will be busy on the wedding day (and not tweeting myself), how can I do this?** You need a head tweeter or a Tweet of Honor (or whatever name you want to call it). You may even want more than one! Create a hashtag for the event and ask these tweeters to tweet before, during, and after the wedding. They need to ask or remind their followers to pass the word around and use the hashtag. They may even tweet celebrities asking them to send out the tweet as well (no guarantees!). This can ultimately be their job on the wedding day. If you are truly making this a social media event, ask the tweeters to visit guests and ask them to tweet or even ask for the words and tweet for them. If you really want to take it over the top, have one of the tweeters read some of the well wishes (at some point) during the reception.

 **Fact**

Some couples are tech savvy and cannot imagine their wedding without it. In fact trending on Twitter sounds like a dream come true and for some the ultimate gift—a gift you cannot buy. Be sure to spread the word of the hashtag on your private groups before the big day too, and then take a shot at being a Twitter superstar for a day.

## Social Media Manager

**I do want my guests to interact via social media; I think it will be cool to see photos and posts about my wedding, but there are so many aspects of social media I am not sure how to manage it.** Surely you have a tech savvy friend—a social media master of sorts. Ask this person if they will be a community manager on the wedding day. This person would be in charge of setting up the laptop and photo/video station for the photo booth, making sure the guests know what the hashtag is on Twitter, relaying user and groups names for other social media outlets, and compiling the posted information after the wedding. Perhaps this is the person responsible for creating a display of the photos and tweets that happened during the wedding and presenting them at the reception.

## Social Media Station

**What is a social media station?** Social media stations are an up and coming trend. It is not quite commonplace yet, but if you are interested in really incorporating social media into the wedding, this is for you. A social media station needs a few basic things: a person to run it, a laptop, and an Internet connection. You can set up your station in a few ways: have guests take photos—think the photo booth trend—and upload the photos directly to Flickr for an instant visual guestbook. You can also ask the guests to tweet at the station, thus having a record of the 140 character (or less) well wishes from the guests—a social media guestbook!

 **Essential**

Don't let social media overpower the real time moments of the wedding. Have the ushers or your community manager pass out cards to the guests with the wedding hashtag, but also with a few notes such as: please refrain from tweeting during the ceremony and please do not post wedding photos until the couple has.

## You Cannot Hide

With the easy access to phones, computers, tablets, and social media, you must realize you cannot control the flow of everything. If you have taken the steps to invite social media into your wedding day, some guests may have a hard time realizing that there is a line that should not be crossed. Someone may make an insensitive comment or post an unflattering photo—that is his downfall, don't let it be yours. Hopefully it won't happen, but you should be prepared.

## You Said What?

**I am concerned someone may make a rude comment about my wedding. Is there anything I can do?** If you choose to put yourself out there by encouraging social media interaction, sadly there may be a person out there somewhere, perhaps that you do not even know who cannot appreciate the fun of it. If you are trying to trend on Twitter there are always trolls (people looking for trouble) who may make unseemly comments. There are those who, no matter what the situation, cannot say anything nice. There is nothing you can do to stop this.

 **Essential**

When you share it all on social media, you may find companies contacting you to provide you with supplies or their product in exchange for links, a mention in your wedding program etc. Do not be lured in by the idea of free stuff. "Sponsored weddings" are the tackiest of all.

## Control the Flow

**I noticed my photographer posts other couple's photos on his Facebook page a lot. I am not sure I feel comfortable with this. Do I have to let him?** You need to speak with your photographer. Ultimately he should not post anything until you have agreed to it and given your approval. Just have a talk with him and explain your concerns, and add a clause to the contract.

**I have had a few interactions with (very distant) friends who are upset they were not invited to the wedding. What should I do?** Even if you "play nice" and use social media appropriately during the planning of your wedding, long lost friends and family members and even mere acquaintances may be upset if they are not included. You simply need to explain that your wedding was for those closest to you. If they continue to give you trouble, it may be time to "unfriend" them!

CHAPTER 6

# The Supporting Cast

*W*hen you announce your engagement, those closest to you will be excited to share in your happiness. Involving your nearest and dearest as members of the wedding party is an honor. Whether it's your best friend, your future sister-in-law, your little sister, or even your mother, these people have signed on to stick with you through the delights and frustrations of wedding planning.

## Selecting the Wedding Party

The wedding party should be a collection of special people from your lives who want nothing more than your happiness. Siblings, good friends, and members of the family are all candidates to be bridesmaids and groomsmen. Just remember to ask people you can lean on for support, who have your best interests at heart, and who are willing to listen to you no matter how important or trivial the planning decisions may be.

### The Numbers Game

**How many attendants should I have?** The number of bridesmaids, groomsmen, and ushers you and your fiancé have is up to you, but in general, the more formal the wedding, the more attendants you have. A good rule of thumb is to have at least one groomsmen or usher for every fifty guests and a corresponding number of bridesmaids.

**Do I need to have the same number of bridesmaids and groomsmen?** It's perfectly okay if you have more bridesmaids than groomsmen, or vice versa. If you're worried about symmetry in the processional or recessional, two groomsmen can always escort one bridesmaid or a bridesmaid can walk out alone. As for the scheduled dances at the reception, you can have one of the "extras" dance with her date or another special guest, or have the entire wedding party dance with their own dates.

 **Fact**

The groomsmen also carry out all the ushers' responsibilities in terms of seating guests and therefore are doing double duty. However, it is entirely appropriate for your fiancé to give the seating duties to his other friends, calling them ushers and thereby enabling even more people to feel like an important part of the wedding ceremony.

## Making Choices

**I have two best friends, and I can't choose between them without the risk of hurt feelings. Can I have two maids of honor?** There is no reason you cannot have two honor attendants. In fact, choosing two maids/matrons of honor should prove beneficial, as the maid of honor duties could be divided between them. As long as you inform both honor attendants of their co-MOH status and help guide them through the task of divvying up responsibilities, you will likely find that two maids are better than one.

**Do I have to include immediate family before friends?** Bridesmaids are supposed to be the people closest to you, so if you haven't talked to your sister since she moved across the country three years ago, there's no rule that states you must have her as a bridesmaid. The same goes for your fiancé's sister. However, not asking them to be in your wedding party may cause family strife, so think twice before excluding them.

## Attendants' Duties

While you may be counting on help from the wedding party, oftentimes the bridesmaids and groomsmen aren't sure what they're supposed to do before or at the wedding. At one time, the bridesmaids' main functions were to guard the bride from evil spirits and bear witness that she was not being forced into marriage against her will, and the best man was charged with the task of keeping potential abductors from absconding with the bride prior to the wedding day. But that was then, this is now, and the attendants have a much more modern set of duties to attend to.

### The Maid of Honor

**What are the maid of honor's duties?** The maid of honor is the bride's legal witness and personal assistant throughout the wedding process. Her more specific duties include:

- Helping the bride with addressing envelopes and recording wedding gifts
- Arranging/hosting a bridal shower
- Assisting with shopping and other pre-wedding tasks
- Collecting funds and organizing a group gift to the bride
- Bringing the groom's ring to the ceremony and holding it until the ring exchange
- Signing the marriage certificate as a witness
- Standing in the receiving line (optional)
- Making a toast (optional)
- Making sure the bride looks perfect for all the pictures
- Dancing with the best man during the attendants' dance at the reception
- Participating in the bouquet toss if single
- Helping the bride change into getaway clothes

## The Bridesmaids

**What are the bridesmaids' duties?** The bridesmaids are an additional support system for the bride and groom. Their specific duties include:

- Assisting the bride and maid of honor with pre-wedding errands and activities
- Helping organize and run the bridal shower
- Assisting the bride in any way on the wedding day
- Participating in the bouquet toss if single
- Standing in the receiving line (optional)

## The Best Man

**What are the best man's duties?** As the groom's legal witness, the best man should help the groom in any way possible. His other duties include:

- Helping the groom get ready and arrive on time for every wedding-related function
- Driving the groom to the ceremony and getting the groom to his wedding on time
- Bringing the bride's ring to the ceremony site
- Giving the officiant his fee immediately before or after the ceremony (provided by the groom's family)
- Holding the bride's ring during the ceremony
- Escorting the maid of honor in the recessional
- Signing the marriage certificate as a witness
- Dancing with the maid of honor during the attendants' dance at the reception
- Proposing the first toast at the reception
- Mingling with the crowd
- Giving other service providers, such as the chauffeur, their fees (optional)
- Assisting with distributing final payments and tips at the wedding

- Driving the couple to the reception and/or the hotel if there is no hired driver
- Overseeing the transfer of gifts to a secure location after the reception
- Returning the groom's attire (if rented)
- Giving the groom moral support, words of wisdom, or assistance of any kind

 **Essential**

The head usher is an optional attendant. He performs and participates in all of the ushers' duties, but is mainly responsible for organizing ushers' activities, and making sure the ushers know their duties and arrive on time on the wedding day.

## The Groomsmen and Ushers

**What are the duties of the groomsmen and ushers?** Like the bridesmaids, the groomsmen are an additional support system for the bride and groom. They participate in pre-wedding festivities and assist the couple on the wedding day. Many times the groomsmen and ushers are one and the same. In larger weddings, additional ushers may be needed to seat the guests. There should be one usher for every fifty guests. Their duties also include:

- Arriving at the wedding location early to help with setup
- Assisting in gathering the wedding party for photographs
- Attending to last-minute tasks such as lighting candles, tying bows on reserved rows of seating, etc.
- Escorting guests to their seats
- Rolling out the aisle runner immediately before the processional
- Directing guests to the reception and handing out pre-printed maps and directions to those who need them

- Collecting discarded programs and articles from the pews after the ceremony
- Helping decorate the newlyweds' car (optional)

## The Mother of the Bride

**Does the mother of the bride have any specific duties?** The mother of the bride is a special position that many mothers look forward to from the moment they give birth to their daughter. It is typical for the mother of the bride to want to be involved and participate in the planning. As an official member of the wedding party, she does have standard duties. These duties include:

- Assisting the bride in selecting her gown, accessories, and trousseau
- Helping the bride select bridesmaids' attire
- Coordinating her attire with the mother of the groom
- Working with the bride, groom, and groom's family to devise a seating plan
- Helping address invitations
- Helping attendants with coordinating the bridal shower
- Assisting the bride with wedding errands and activities
- Standing in the receiving line
- Acting as hostess of the reception

# The Little Ones

For some, having children be a part of the wedding is a must. Others would prefer to give it no thought at all. Whether you choose to include the little ones in the wedding party is entirely up to you.

## Guidelines

**What are the age guidelines for flower girls, ring bearers, and junior bridesmaids?** Junior bridesmaids are usually between ten and fourteen, while flower girls are younger, between four and nine. Little boys, usually under ten, can be ring bearers. Other little boys and girls, called trainbearers, can walk behind the bride, carrying her train.

**Can I have attendants of different sexes?** This is quite common in modern weddings. If your best friend is a male, and he's taking the place of your maid of honor, he's called the honor attendant; if not, he's simply another attendant. Also, if your fiancé has a female attendant she's still called an usher or a groomsperson, but she shouldn't escort female guests to their seats.

## Responsibilities

**Do I need to have a flower girl and a ring bearer? If so, what are their responsibilities?** Etiquette does not dictate that you must have either at your wedding. These roles are there for the purpose of incorporating children in your ceremony. In general, young family members are chosen as a flower girl or ring bearer. The flower child walks down the aisle ahead of the bride and scatters flower petals at her feet. The ring bearer carries a velvet cushion or silver tray on which the (stand-in) wedding bands are held until needed.

**My older sister is my matron of honor, but I also want to include my twelve-year-old sister as an honor attendant. How would I go about doing this?** Recognizing your younger sister is a great idea. Girls of junior bridesmaid age who are given an honor position are called maidens of honor. While you can't count on your younger sister to plan the wedding shower and the bachelorette party, including her along with your older sister should make her feel included and an active participant in the wedding.

## Attendant Dilemmas

Though it may be hard to believe, some people will not be thrilled at the prospect of being included in a wedding. Others may turn down this opportunity due to personal or financial reasons. If this happens to you, be gracious and understanding. Most importantly, don't let if affect your relationship. Your friend probably has a good reason for declining your offer.

## Attendant Protocol

**Am I supposed to pay for lodging for out-of-town attendants?** If your attendants are coming from a distance to be in your wedding, you should try to arrange for them to stay with another friend or family member. If alternate housing is not available, you should pay for rooms at a nearby hotel. But if your attendant would rather stay at a hotel than with your Aunt Martha, she should pay for the hotel herself.

**Is it okay to have an honor attendant who lives out of town?** While the honor attendant does have considerable responsibilities before the wedding, you shouldn't let distance be a deciding factor. Keep in mind that an out-of town maid of honor won't be there to help you with as much pre-wedding planning as would someone who lives locally, but with modern technology she can still do quite a lot.

## Fulfilling the Duties

**I have a close friend whom I would love to make a bridesmaid. Unfortunately, she has a tendency to act irresponsibly. What should I do?** If you have doubts about the dependability of any of the friends and family on your list of potential wedding party members, think twice before you ask them. It could be an awful strain on the relationship if you had to take back your offer because someone turned out to be more of a headache than a help. If you do find yourself in the position of having to rescind an offer, if possible, do it before the friend purchases her dress or makes travel arrangements, or be prepared to reimburse her for her expenses. Again, be prepared for this to cause some strife in the relationship; in fact, depending on the circumstances, you may just want to continue to include her but not rely on her for any formal duties.

**What do I do if one of my attendants isn't fulfilling her duties?** Give her the benefit of the doubt. When it comes to fulfilling their duties, most attendants are waiting for cues from the bride. Perhaps you could create a list of attendants' duties that you would specifically like assistance with, including target dates for completing these duties. Go about this in a fun way, not as if you are the queen. If even this doesn't work, try talking to her. Maybe she has other things going on in her life that are preventing her from helping you out. But unless her behavior is extreme, you're going to have to just grin and bear it.

## It Costs How Much?

**How do I respond if a friend says no because she can't afford it?** If she's a really good friend and it's in your budget, you could offer to pay for a portion or all of her expenses. Just don't let the other bridesmaids know, or they could go on strike and demand payment for their dresses, too. Your other option is to give her a part in your wedding that is less costly, like that of a reader.

# CHAPTER 7

# Playing Dress Up

*Y*our walk down the aisle is one of the grandest moments of your life, and without a doubt you should look and feel your best. While the formality of the wedding will influence many of your decisions, that does not mean you cannot inject some style and personality into your look. But it is not all about you! Your fiancé, the wedding party, and your parents are part of the wedding package, and they are looking to make a stylish statement themselves.

## The When, What, and Why of Dress

The all-important decision regarding the formality of your wedding influences all other planning decisions. The formality of the wedding is instrumental in completing the look and achieving the vision you desire. Traditional guidelines will get you moving in the right direction, but this is the twenty-first century and modern brides and grooms are forging their own paths.

### Formal

**What are the guidelines for a formal wedding?** The traditional guidelines for a formal wedding are as follows:

- Ceremony held in a church, synagogue, or luxury hotel
- Reception held in a luxury hotel, private club, or private estate
- 100 or more guests

- Engraved or printed invitations with traditional wording
- The bride wears a floor-length gown with a chapel-length or sweeping train, fingertip veil or hat, and gloves
- The groom wears a cutaway or tails
- Bride and groom each have between three and six attendants
- Bridesmaids wear floor-length gowns
- Male attendants wear matching cutaways or tails
- Guests wear formal attire or evening wear
- Sit-down dinner
- Live entertainment
- Elaborate floral and event design
- Luxury transportation

 **Fact**

Very formal weddings follow the same guidelines as formal weddings but with a heightened sense of formality and drama. Expect that a very formal wedding would have 200 or more guests, between four and twelve attendants each, and a white-tie dress code. The bride's dress, the wedding party's attire, and the guests' attire should reflect this very formal style.

## Semiformal

**What constitutes a semiformal wedding?** The traditional guidelines for a semiformal wedding are as follows:
- Held in a church, synagogue, private home, or outdoors
- Reception held at ceremony location, club, garden, restaurant, hotel, or home
- Fewer than 100 guests
- Invitations may be printed with traditional or personalized wording

- The bride wears a floor- or cocktail-length gown with a fingertip veil or hat
- The groom wears a tuxedo, sack coat, or a suit and tie
- Bride and groom each have between one and three attendants
- Bridesmaids wear matching floor- or cocktail-length dresses
- Male attendants wear matching tuxes or suits and ties
- Guests wear evening or business dress
- Meal can be anything from sit-down to buffet to light refreshments
- Live band or disc jockey
- Scaled-down floral arrangements and event design

## Informal

**What constitutes an informal wedding?** The traditional guidelines for an informal wedding are as follows:

- Daytime ceremonies held at a home, community center, hotel, or in a judge's chambers
- Fewer than fifty guests
- Printed or hand-written invitations with personalized wording
- The bride wears a simple gown, suit, or cocktail-length dress with no veil or train
- The groom wears a dark business suit and tie
- Bride and groom each have one attendant
- Maid/matron of honor wears a street-length dress
- Best man wears a suit and tie
- Reception usually held at a home, ceremony site, or a restaurant
- Simple meal or light refreshments are served
- Simple floral designs

## New Rules for Weddings

**Do I have to follow these traditional guidelines when planning my wedding?** With these traditional guidelines in mind, you must remember that this is the new millennium and originality reigns supreme. A meticulously planned reception with crystal chandeliers, amazing floral arrangements, the best photographer money can buy, and a $7,000 gown can easily take place on a rustic ranch. Do you call that formal or informal? That's the beauty of the creativity today's brides, wedding planners, and designers bring to the table. Let your wedding speak for you and be a reflection of you.

## The Bride

Chances are your wedding gown is the most important—and expensive—piece of clothing you'll ever buy. There is an enormous amount of pressure to find that "perfect" gown, and while at times is may seem like you are lost in a maze of white dresses, by taking your time and shopping wisely you will find the right dress for you.

## Let's Shop!

**How soon should I start shopping for my wedding gown?** You can begin your search at any time, but eight to twelve months before the wedding is fine timing. This provides ample time to shop, compare, and order the gown. Keep in mind that wedding gowns should be ordered about six months before the wedding, so don't put off shopping for too long. If you're considering having a gown made, begin your process around the twelve-month mark to ensure you will find a designer that can produce your custom-made creation within your time frame.

**What should I bring with me when shopping for my gown?** Bring the proper undergarments: a strapless bra or bustier, shoes (in a heel height you typically wear), and any "must wear" jewelry or accessories. You may end up replacing some of these items with others, but it does give you a good idea of what to expect.

 **Alert**

Many religions require that certain areas of the body be covered or that veils be worn during the ceremony. Before you go shopping, check with your ceremony venue and your officiant to determine whether there are any restrictions or special regulations for your gown. Also be sure to ask about restrictions on attire for the rest of the wedding party.

**My fiancé's mother was hurt that I didn't bring her along to look for my gown. Was I wrong in excluding her?** There are no rules about who should go gown shopping with you. You can always ask your mother-in-law to accompany you to one of your fittings. Most brides ask their mother or maid of honor to accompany them. Most importantly, your shopping companions should be supportive, helpful, and honest. It makes no difference if this person is part of your wedding party.

## Fashionable Mentions

**I found a gown with a cathedral-length train that I absolutely adore. Is this appropriate for an afternoon outdoor ceremony?** Basically, the length of the gown's train and veil determines how formal the gown is. Long, cathedral-length trains are best suited for a very formal evening wedding, while shorter chapel or sweep trains are appropriate for less formal daytime or evening weddings.

**What are the styles of trains?** You need to look at the length and style of the train when determining which overall look best suits your wedding. Trains may be attached, requiring a bustle for the reception. Others are detachable and may be removed completely.

**Train Styles**
- The royal is a dramatic and extravagant train and falls up to twelve feet on the floor.
- The cathedral train is a very formal length. It falls anywhere from six to eight feet on the floor.
- The chapel train is a popular choice among brides. It falls three to four feet on the floor.
- The court is less formal than a chapel train. It falls about a foot onto the floor.
- The sweep is less formal, falling around six inches on the floor.
- The watteau falls from the shoulder blades or back yoke to the floor.

## Dress Dilemmas

**I'm a forty-year-old bride. This will be the first marriage for both my fiancé and for me. Can I still wear a traditional white gown?** Any first-time bride can wear a formal, white wedding gown. What is important is to select a gown that is appropriate for your age and the formality of the wedding.

 **Essential**

A current trend is for the bride to have two gowns, one for the ceremony and formal photos and one for the reception or party. The gowns are usually very different in style and feel to reflect the two components of the wedding day.

**As a first-time bride, is it in bad taste for me to wear a colored gown?** Color is not only appropriate, it is a fashion statement. Older relatives and guests may question this decision because it is not what they are accustomed to. Designers offer many options in soft, appropriate wedding colors. You can add color as accents on sashes, rosettes, and lace/appliqué details. Another option is to wear a traditional white gown, but add a sash, wrap, or brooch with a dash of color at the reception.

**I love my mother's wedding gown and think it would be an honor to wear it. However, my parents are divorced. Would this be inappropriate?** You first need to ask your mother how she feels about this. She may not be interested in dredging up old memories quite yet; if that is the case, wearing her wedding gown would be inconsiderate. If your mother is on board, then it is really a fine thing to do. A wedding gown is a sentimental and ceremonial garment, and the status of your parents' relationship should not define or diminish the meaning of the gown.

## Accessories

**Is it necessary to wear a veil over my face?** The veil that covers the face is called a blusher. In most cases, it isn't necessary. However, some religions do require that the face be covered at some point during the ceremony, so check with your officiant.

**Do I need to wear a veil?** Just to be clear, blushers and veils are not synonymous; you may wear a veil without the blusher. Unless your religious affiliation requires it, both are completely optional. Many brides wear a veil for the ceremony and remove it for the reception. If you choose to forego the veil, try a dazzling headpiece, crystal hairpins, or fresh flowers to complete your wedding-day ensemble.

**Should I wear gloves with a sleeveless gown?** Traditionally, elbow-length gloves are worn if the gown has short sleeves or is sleeveless. Short gloves are worn otherwise. However, gloves are optional and many brides choose to forego the gloves altogether.

If you decide to wear elbow-length gloves, split the seam of the glove so you can easily get your ring finger out (the seam can be re-stitched later). If you wear short gloves, take one off during the exchanging of rings. If you choose to wear your gloves during the reception, they can be left on at all times except when you're eating.

 **Essential**

> Don't forget your "something old, something new, something borrowed, something blue." The old represents ties to the past; the new, hope for the future; the borrowed, friendship; and the blue, faithfulness.

## Alterations

**Do all gowns need alterations?** Most gowns will need some sort of alterations in order to fit you perfectly. The bridal consultant should present you with an estimate or pricing chart for alterations when you order your gown. Be sure to ask about costs for adding bustles or any other alterations that may need to be done.

## The Bridesmaids

Brides are famous for proclaiming, "You can wear it again." While the bridesmaids may not actually be able to wear it again, at least the days of ugly dresses are over. As any glance through a bridal magazine will show you, bridesmaids' dresses can be tasteful, elegant, and fashion-forward.

## Selecting the Dress

**Was I wrong to not solicit my bridesmaids' opinions before selecting their dresses?** You do not have to consult with the ladies about the dress. This is your wedding and it should reflect your taste. Of course, you can take their opinions into consideration, but they don't have final approval over what they wear.

**Can I just let my bridesmaids select their own dresses?** If you're having a hard time finding a dress that looks great on all of your bridesmaids, don't send them off shopping on their own. Instead, look for a designer that offers coordinating separates with varying necklines, waistlines, and sleeve lengths. This way all of the dresses will be in the same fabric and the same length to ensure there is some uniformity and cohesion in the overall look.

## Color Correction

**Can bridesmaids wear black?** At one time black was considered inappropriate for weddings. However, now it is a chic fashion statement. Many designers offer black as a standard color option. If your mother is traditional or even superstitious you may want to consult her on the matter.

**Should junior bridesmaids wear the same dress as the bridesmaids?** A junior bridesmaid can wear the same dress as the other bridesmaids as long as it is appropriate for her age. If the bridesmaids' dresses are not appropriate, then a dress in the same color and fabric but in a more appropriate style would be in order.

## The Groom and His Men

In choosing wedding attire, men experience considerably less stress than their female counterparts. That's because, quite simply, they don't really have as many choices to make. Your wedding's style generally dictates what your fiancé and his ushers will wear, but, of course, nothing is written in stone.

## Shopping for Formalwear

**When should my fiancé reserve his clothing?** Your fiancé and the other men in the wedding party should go to a formalwear shop at least three to four months before the wedding in order to reserve their attire and ensure the shop can accommodate your stylistic decisions.

**Should my fiancé just buy a tuxedo?** That really depends on your lifestyle. If you think that there will be an occasion to wear one within the next couple of years, it may be worth the money. If he does decide to purchase instead of rent, make sure he finds a classic style that won't be dated in a few years.

**What if one of the ushers lives in another city or state?** He should go to a tuxedo shop in his area to be measured and then pass that information along to the groom so that his tuxedo can be reserved along with the rest of the ushers'. Formalwear rental chains with locations across the country can help you coordinate this; just make sure they carry a tuxedo you like.

## Formalwear 101

**Should each tuxedo or suit match exactly?** All the men in the wedding party should wear the same style and color attire. The groom often wears a different color tie/bowtie and cummerbund/vest than the rest of the men.

**What should the little guys wear?** Junior ushers, ring bearers, and pages should match the rest of the men in the wedding party. The younger boys can also wear dress shorts or knickers. Do remember that a four-year-old may not be comfortable in a mini-tuxedo; children of that age can wear coordinated children's clothing instead.

# The Parents

Work with your parents to find attire that will allow them each to look their best and to shine—but not outshine you—on your wedding day.

## Must They Match?

**Are the mothers' dresses supposed to match?** The mothers' dresses don't have to match exactly, but they should be complementary in color, style, and length.

## Color Coded

**My fiancé's mother wants to wear a white dress! How can I tell her I'd prefer her to wear a different color?** Unless you're having a white wedding where everyone is requested to wear white or a very light color, the mothers of the bride and groom shouldn't wear white. That color is reserved for the bride and sometimes the flower girl. Talk to your future mother-in-law about her color choice.

## Perfectly Styled

**Should the fathers' clothes match the other men in the wedding party?** The style and color of the fathers' clothes should match that of the other male attendants. They can be differentiated with their accessories. For example, if the groomsmen are wearing vests instead of cummerbunds, the fathers can wear cummerbunds. Alternately, if the groomsmen are wearing colored accessories to match the bridesmaids, the fathers can opt for simple black accessories.

## Proper Fit

**When and where should the dads get their formal-wear?**
They should get their wedding attire at the same formalwear shop as your fiancé and his wedding party about three to four months before the wedding. If your father or your fiancé's father lives out of town, he should give his measurements to you so his tuxedo can be ordered along with the others. If by some chance your dad already owns a tuxedo and wants to wear it, have him pull it out and try it on. If it is acceptable to you, have it cleaned and pressed and purchase or rent the coordinating accessories.

# CHAPTER 8

# Spectacular Soirées

*Y*our glorious vision is beginning to come to life. You've chosen your bridesmaids, tackled the guest list, and convinced your father that a backyard barbecue wasn't exactly the kind of reception you had in mind. As the wedding day draws nearer, it is time to create your bridal registry and start thinking about the other festivities that go hand-in-hand with a wedding celebration.

## Who Are All These People?

Your mother wants to invite her walking buddy, who knows everything about your wedding despite the fact that she's never met you. Your mother-in-law wants to invite the ladies from the country club, because she was invited to all of their daughters' weddings. You're just wondering, "How do I make sense of all these people, keep everyone happy, and not lose my mind?"

### Why Have a Bridal Shower?

**What is the bridal shower for?** A bridal shower is a time for close friends and family to celebrate a couple's impending marriage and, of course, to shower the couple with gifts.

**Is it necessary to invite every woman from the guest list to the bridal shower?** Showers are supposed to be small and intimate, so there's no need to invite every female on the wedding guest list. Only close friends of the bride and family members need to be included.

**Many of my close friends live out of town. Should they be invited to the shower even though I know they won't be able to attend?** Sending a shower invitation to friends in distant places is a great way to make them feel included in the festivities. Long-distance invitations should be extended only to those with whom you have a close relationship, as these guests may feel compelled to send gifts and you do not want the invitation to seem like you are just looking for gifts.

 Question

Is it okay to have more than one bridal shower?
Many brides have more than one shower to accommodate different groups of invitees. A distant member of the groom's family or a coworker may want to host a shower. Dividing the guest list can also lessen the financial burden one large bridal shower can impose on the hostess.

## Special Considerations

**If most of my close friends, including my maid of honor, live out of town, can they throw a shower the day before the wedding?** Throwing the shower in the days before the wedding is a viable option. Just be sure this last-minute bridal shower doesn't conflict with other wedding activities, such as the bridesmaids' tea, wedding rehearsal, or the rehearsal dinner.

**Can we have a co-ed party instead?** There's no reason you can't have a co-ed party; just try to avoid gender-specific activities and bridal shower games. Stick to a gender-neutral theme as well.

# The Bridal Shower

After all the planning you have done—and still have to do—when it comes time for the bridal shower, you get to relax and let others take the reins. Your input, however, should be solicited for some matters, such as the theme and guest list. But for the most part, you can sit back and enjoy the shower; this is the time for you to be feted without having to worry about so much as one logistical detail.

## Hosting Duties

**In regard to the bridal shower, what are the bride's responsibilities?** The bride is expected to help the maid of honor by compiling a guest list, offering an opinion about the shower's theme, and providing her with the names and locations of the stores where you're registered.

 **Fact**

Etiquette dictates that a member of the bride's immediate family should not host a bridal shower. However, this is now commonplace, as many women choose to have their sister as their honor attendant. Traditionally, the honor attendant is responsible for planning and hosting the bridal shower.

**Can my mother host a wedding shower?** Traditionally, your mother or grandmother should not host a shower; that responsibility should be left to more distant relatives, like a cousin or aunt, or to the maid of honor, bridesmaids, and other friends. The logic behind this rule is that the bride and groom's families shouldn't appear to be asking for gifts. This same rule applies to the groom's immediate family hosting a shower.

**Is it okay for my coworkers to plan a shower for me, even if they are not invited to the wedding?** Even if you couldn't invite them to the big event, it is perfectly acceptable to allow them to throw you a shower. Normally, the coworker shower is thrown on one of your last days at work prior to the wedding. Colleagues typically gather during the lunch hour or right after work for refreshments and the presentation of a group gift.

## Who's Invited?

**What is the suggested wording for bridal shower invitations?** The following is a sample of standard wording for a bridal shower invitation:

Please join us for
A bridal shower in honor of
Jaclyn Marie Nelson
on Sunday, the twenty-fifth of June
at one o'clock in the afternoon
The Restaurant
123 West Fifth Avenue
Los Angeles, California
R.S.V.P. by June 5
Alice Buckley, (555) 123-4567

**Should some guests be invited to more than one shower?** The only people who should be invited to more than one shower are the bride and groom's mothers and the attendants. They shouldn't be expected to buy presents for each shower—just one will suffice.

**Can we invite guests to the shower who aren't invited to the wedding?** With few exceptions, you shouldn't. But if you're having a small wedding or a destination wedding and your friends decide to throw you a shower anyway, that's fine.

**Is my fiancé allowed at the shower?** Most men are really not interested in attending the bridal shower, but if he does want to pop in, ask him to join you for the gift opening.

## Being Gracious

**What can I do to show my appreciation to the people who throw a bridal shower?** For those who are kind enough to throw parties in your honor, show your gratitude by sending both a thank-you note and a small gift.

**I know it's proper to write thank-you notes for wedding presents, but what about shower presents?** Whenever you receive a present, a thank-you note should be sent as a show of appreciation.

 **Fact**

> A thank-you note should include a mention of the gift, how you plan to use it, and a personal statement or comment such as, "It was lovely of you to come so far to be a part of the bridal shower." If the gift was monetary or a gift card, a reference to the amount is optional, but you should mention how you plan to use the money.

## Bridesmaids' Teas

Honor your bridesmaids with a traditional bridesmaids' tea. This is a fun and intimate gathering of your closest friends. It is a great way to show them how much you appreciate their support, and to thank them for their friendship.

**What is a bridesmaids' tea?** The bridesmaids' tea, held on the weekend or in the days prior to the wedding, is an opportunity for the bride to show her gratitude to the bridesmaids and treat them to a celebration. This is a great time to present the ladies with their attendants' gifts as well. This is an event for the bridesmaids only; however, mothers have been known to attend.

**Are there any other options for taking the bridesmaids out?** The tea doesn't have to be a tea in the technical sense. It can be any type of event you want it to be. Lunch, a spa day, cocktails and hors d'oeuvres, wine tasting, or dinner are other options.

## The Bridal Registry

Many guests have come to rely on modern bridal registries when looking for that perfect gift. Guests will use the registry to purchase gifts for the bridal shower as well as for the wedding. The items on the registry should include essential items that you and your fiancé feel are needed for your life together.

## Why Register?

**Why should I register?** The idea of a bridal registry is to provide the bride with a trousseau, or the things she and her husband will probably need during their first year as a married couple. It is also your opportunity to provide your guests with some guidance when it comes to gift giving.

**Am I supposed to enclose the registry cards with all of my invitations?** Some salespeople/consultants mistakenly tell you to put the registry cards in all of your invitations. While it is acceptable to include this information with shower invitations, it is not okay to enclose these cards with engagement party or wedding invitations, as a gift is not a requirement for either of these events.

## Preparing the Registry

**How do I start my bridal registry?** First, you and your fiancé should sit down and decide what items you need or would like to register for; many stores (and their websites) offer complete lists to aid in this process. You will also want to discuss colors, styles, and preferences for housewares and décor. Once you have some of these details in place, you can decide which stores are right for you to register at and then officially establish your registries. This will enter you into the store's system and make your selections available for viewing by your guests.

Be considerate of all your guests by registering for items that cover a range of budgets. Be sure to include items in the twenty-dollar price range as well as place settings of china and silver. If you are registering at an upscale store, consider a second registry at a medium-priced store as well.

**Do we need to register for formal china, silver, and crystal?** You do not need to register for anything you do not feel you would use or need. You should take into account, however, that while certain items, such as formal china, may seem ridiculous now, it may not in five or ten years when you have the family over for a holiday meal. Formal china and the components that go hand-in-hand with it—crystal and silver—are investments, and it doesn't hurt to have wedding guests who can afford and want to purchase these items help you in acquiring them.

## The Traditional Registry

**What should I include on a traditional registry?** The traditional bridal registry should include essentials for the home. Be sure to register for an adequate number of items. For example, you should include between eight to twelve place settings each of china, silverware, and crystal—enough to accommodate the guests at a dinner party or holiday meal.

**Bed Linens**
- ❑ Fitted sheets
- ❑ Flat sheets
- ❑ Pillowcases
- ❑ Pillows
- ❑ Blankets
- ❑ Mattress pad or cover
- ❑ Bedspread or comforter

**Table Linens**
- ❑ Formal napkins
- ❑ Formal tablecloth
- ❑ Informal napkins
- ❑ Informal place mats
- ❑ Cotton or pad liner for tablecloth
- ❑ Smaller tablecloths and napkins

**Bath Linens**
- ❑ Large bath towels
- ❑ Hand towels
- ❑ Face cloths
- ❑ Bath mat or rug
- ❑ Shower curtain
- ❑ Small guest towels

**Cookware**
- ❑ Frying pan
- ❑ Covered saucepans (large and small)
- ❑ Tea kettle
- ❑ Utensil set
- ❑ Baking pans

**China (formal and everyday)**
- ❑ Dinner plates
- ❑ Salad plates
- ❑ Cups and saucers
- ❑ Creamer and sugar bowl

- ❏ Salt and pepper shakers
- ❏ Soup bowls
- ❏ Bread and butter plates
- ❏ Serving platters
- ❏ Glassware/crystal
- ❏ Water goblets
- ❏ Wine glasses
- ❏ Cocktail glasses
- ❏ Champagne glasses

**Silverware (formal and everyday)**
- ❏ Knives
- ❏ Dinner forks
- ❏ Salad forks
- ❏ Soup spoons
- ❏ Teaspoons

**Silverware (additions to formal service)**
- ❏ Butter knife
- ❏ Fish knife
- ❏ Dessert fork
- ❏ Shrimp fork
- ❏ Iced tea spoon
- ❏ Steak knife
- ❏ Carving knife
- ❏ Slotted spoon
- ❏ Pie server
- ❏ Gravy boat and spoon
- ❏ Chafing dishes

## Beyond China and Towels

When it comes to bridal registries, brides and grooms never had it so good. You name it, you can probably register for it. You are no longer locked in to selecting only china, silver, crystal, and bath towels. When it comes to creating a modern trousseau, look at your lifestyle and interests and find the right stores for your needs.

**Is it true you can register for your honeymoon?** A honeymoon registry is a service that is offered, usually for a fee, by national travel companies and some local travel agents. To do this, you create an account, decide on your honeymoon destination and what you would like to include in the registry, including airfare, hotel accommodation, and meals. You may also select additional activities for your honeymoon like snorkeling, private dinners, massages, and moonlight cruises. Guests help you purchase the honeymoon by contributing to this registry. The service should provide you with a list of all contributors and their gifts to facilitate sending thank-you notes.

**A photographer suggested we set up a registry for our wedding photographs. Is this common?** As couples' eyes get bigger than their pocketbooks, both vendors and couples are looking for new ways to cash in on their guests' generosity. Ultra-conservative etiquette "laws" may frown on such a registry because it seems a little less than kosher to have guests partially finance the couple's wedding budget. Ultimately, only you can decide what is right for you.

 **Essential**

Organizations like the I Do Foundation (*www.idofoundation.com*) allow you to choose a charity guests can donate to in your name in lieu of gifts. It's also possible to set up a traditional registry through the I Do Foundation where a percentage of the amount of money your guests spend on your gift will go to the charity of your choice.

**Is registering with my favorite local shop a bad idea?** If you have a local independent shop that you just love, ask them if they already have a registry or if they will set one up for you. It may be as simple as making a list of gift items. Just be aware that if you have a lot of out-of-town guests and the store does not have online shopping, you may not receive many items from this registry, but any local guests will certainly benefit. Many independent stores will be willing to take phone orders for people purchasing off of a registry and will be able to give your guests the individual attention that may be lacking at larger chain stores.

CHAPTER 9

# The Paper Trail

*Y*our wedding is coming to life, and it is about to be in print. The invitation ensemble you select speaks volumes about the tone, style, and formality of your big day. While the invitation is a guest's first glimpse into your wedding festivities, it is by no means the beginning or end of the paper trail. From elegant and engraved to one-of-a-kind customized creations, make sure your selections give the guests the right impression of your celebration.

## Mark Your Calendars

Once upon a time, someone had the brilliant idea that brides should let their guests know they are planning a wedding. Since then, Save-the-Date cards have made it possible for guests from all over the globe to clear their schedules and celebrate wonderful weddings with their nearest and dearest. If only all things were this convenient!

### Save the Date

**What is a Save-the-Date?** Save-the-Dates are mailings that let the guests know a wedding is being planned for a particular date. These cards have become immensely popular because they give family and friends living around the world a little heads-up that an important event is coming. Keep in mind that a Save-the-Date is not an invitation to anything; it is merely a precursor to the invitation, giving the guests time to make travel arrangements.

**Fact**

**Can I e-mail a Save-the-Date?** You can if your wedding is ultra-casual. The Save-the-Date is like a movie trailer; it is a preview of your wedding. Therefore, its formality and tone should reflect the overall tone of the wedding.

## Wording

**What is the wording for a Save-the-Date?** The basic wording is simple and includes the bride and groom's names, sometimes the host's name, the date of the wedding, and the geographic location of the wedding. You may also include travel, tourist, and accommodation information. This is also a good chance to direct guests to your wedding website.

> Save the Date
> for the marriage of
> Christine Smith
> and
> Arthur Jones
> July 11, 2012
> Los Angeles, California
> Formal invitation to follow

# Invitations 101

An invitation is an invitation. How hard can it be? Think again. There are typestyles, ink colors, printing options, paper weights, and more. The wedding invitation is a unique ensemble made of many components that all work in sync with one another. A crash course on the details that go into creating your invitation ensemble awaits.

## The Wedding Invitation

**When should I order my invitations?** Your invitations should be ordered about four to six months in advance. This will allow enough time for you to have the order processed, receive the order, and have the invitations assembled and addressed. If you are considering custom-designed invitations, you should allow yourself more time to account for the design process.

 **Essential**

Custom-designed invitations are pricey, but you can still achieve a designer look at a fraction of the cost by using standard invitation books. Beautiful envelope liners, modern typestyles, a variety of design motifs and monograms, and a large range of ink colors are available to customize your invitations. You can also accomplish this with ribbons, charms, and other accessories.

**Other than engraved invitations, what options do I have?** There are four common printing methods for invitations. They include:

- **Engraving:** Viewed as the most formal, they are also one of the most expensive options. A plate of the invitation is made and the paper is pressed onto it, raising the print, on which a layer of ink is then applied.

- **Letterpress:** In essence, this is the reverse process of engraving; a plate is pressed into the paper from on top, leaving the letters depressed into the card. These invitations are fairly equivalent in price to engraved invitations.
- **Thermography:** This is an extremely popular and cost effective option that offers a similar look to an engraved invitation. Ink and powder are fused together, giving the letters a raised appearance on the front of the invitation.
- **Lithography or Offset Printing:** This is a flat printing process that is the least expensive printing option.

## The Components

**What are the components of the invitation?** The components of the basic wedding invitation include:

- **Invitation:** Invites the guest to the wedding and provides the necessary details: bride and groom's names, host, date, time, and ceremony location.
- **Response Card and Envelope:** Allows the guests to indicate whether or not they'll be attending and if they're bringing a guest (if a guest is invited). Traditional etiquette dictates a guest is to write her own reply to the host, but pre-printed response cards have become the norm.
- **Reception Card:** Directs the guests to the location of the reception. If the ceremony and reception are in the same location, a reception card is not always necessary. You may print "Reception immediately follows" in the lower left corner of the invitation.
- **Map or Direction Card:** Provides guests with the address and driving directions to the wedding venue.
- **Inner Envelope:** Part of a traditional presentation, it is becoming common to skip it in favor of saving paper. The

stacked and completed invitation ensemble is inserted into the inner envelope with the text facing the back flap.

- **Outer Envelope:** The complete invitation, whether inserted into the inner envelope or stacked on its own, is placed inside this envelope to be stamped and mailed. The return address should be printed on the back flap of this outer envelope.

 Essential

Do not forget to pre-stamp the response card envelope. This facilitates the process of promptly receiving your response cards. Make responding as easy as you can for the guests and you can expect to have an easier time solidifying a guest count.

## Ordering the Invitations

**What do we need to know or do before we order the invitations?** To make the ordering process easier, keep a few key points in mind.

1. Know how many invitations you need. You can usually count one invitation per household.

2. Have an idea about the wording of your invitation. Will your parents' names appear on the invitation? What about your fiancé's parents? Will you be using a poem or verse or other unique wording?

3. Confirm and reconfirm the details. Be sure you have the correct ceremony start time, the correct spellings of all people and locations, and the address for the ceremony and reception.

4. Know your response deadline, usually two to three weeks prior to the wedding. If you are using an R.S.V.P. service, you will need the company's designated phone number and website information.

**5.** Know if you are providing guests with a meal choice; you will need to have this indicated on the response card.

**Can we cut costs by omitting postage from the response cards?** It is not recommended because it facilitates the response process. You can cut down on the cost of postage by making your response card a postcard.

**Can we use a phone number for our responses instead of a card?** If your wedding is casual or invitations are going out last minute, it can be acceptable. If you are looking to skip the mailing of response cards altogether, try an R.S.V.P. service. For a fee, the company tracks the responses via a toll-free phone number (usually with a personal extension) or a website address for the guests to call/send in their responses. This is not a traditional reply method, so some of your guests may be a little confused. It is a personal choice; some brides love this idea and others are appalled. You will still need to include a card to convey the information. The following is a sample:

Please respond by June 25, 2012
(Name of Service), 1-888-555-2012
Website address

## What (and What Not) to Say

We all know that you're not supposed to list where you're registered on the wedding invitation, right? Good! But many couples encounter situations that they feel might merit a quick mention on the wedding invitations. However, with few exceptions, nothing but the standard date, time, and location of the ceremony should be listed on the actual invitation.

## By the Way . . .

**How can we let guests know we'd prefer black tie?** The words "Black Tie Invited" at the bottom of your invitation will let guests know that you're planning a formal wedding. However, you can't mandate tuxedoes, suits, or any other type of dress.

**Can we write "No Smoking" on the wedding invitation or reception card?** While it's okay to forbid smoking at your reception, you shouldn't print that on the invitation. Just leave the ashtrays off the tables, place small "No Smoking" cards on each table, and be sure the wait staff knows your wishes. Depending on your venue, smoking may not be allowed or may only be allowed in designated areas.

 **Essential**

Strictly speaking, "The honor of your presence is requested" is wording reserved for those getting married in a house of worship. If your wedding is not at a house of worship, try "You are cordially invited" or "Request the pleasure of your company" instead.

**Is there a way to indicate on the invitation that children aren't desired at the wedding?** This should not be indicated on the invitation; it is implied by the inclusion or exclusion of the child's name on either the outer or inner envelope. If the child's name is excluded, the parents should understand that children aren't invited. However, not everybody will get these subtle hints, so be sure that your mother and anyone else who may be asked are aware of your policy.

## Gifts Galore

**How can I let people know where we are registered?** Registry information should not be included with the wedding invitation. Have your mother, future mother-in-law, wedding party, and other family members pass that information along when and if they are asked what you would like or where you are registered. Posting that information on your wedding website is also acceptable.

**Some of my guests are not in a position to buy gifts. Can I request that people not buy us gifts by printing "No gifts, please" on the invitation?** Such a request is not proper on an invitation. A handwritten note to specific guests will do the job. For example, "We look forward to seeing you at our wedding, and we are asking our friends not to bring gifts. Your presence in itself will be as fine a gift as we can imagine."

## You Are Cordially Invited

The rules for wording the wedding invitation are evolving as quickly as the etiquette that applies to invitations. Most importantly the invitation informs the guests of the vital logistical information, including the who, what, when, and where. However, keep in mind the wording and style of the invitation says a lot about the wedding's formality and style.

### Wording the Invitation

**How do I know what wording I should use for my invitation?** The following are samples of basic invitation wording for many common circumstances. Quotes, poems, and other specialized wording may be added to invitations as well. Use these samples as a guideline for determining your wording.

**Traditional**
Mr. and Mrs. Joseph Dye
request the honor of your presence
at the marriage of their daughter
Jaclyn Ann
to
Mr. Arthur Jackson

Saturday, the eleventh of July
two thousand twelve
at three o'clock in the afternoon
Holy Trinity Lutheran Church
New York, New York

### Bride and Groom's Parents Sponsor

Mr. and Mrs. Joseph Dye
and
Mr. and Mrs. Robert Jackson
request the honor of your presence
at the marriage of their children
Miss Jaclyn Ann Dye
and
Mr. Arthur James Jackson

### Traditional: Bride's Parents Sponsor, Groom's Parents Listed

Mr. and Mrs. Joseph Dye
request the honor of your presence
at the marriage of their daughter
Jaclyn Ann
to
Mr. Arthur Jackson
son of
Mr. and Mrs. Robert Jackson

### Groom's Parents Host

Mr. and Mrs. Robert Jackson
request the honor of your presence
at the marriage of
Miss Jaclyn Ann Dye
to their son
Mr. Arthur James Jackson

### Bride and Groom Host

The honor of your presence is requested
at the marriage of
Miss Jaclyn Ann Dye
and
Mr. Arthur James Jackson
or
Miss Jaclyn Ann Dye
and
Mr. Arthur James Jackson
request the honor of your presence
at their marriage

### Bride's Mother Hosts

Mrs. Patricia Dye
requests the honor of your presence
at the marriage of her daughter
Jaclyn Ann

### Bride's Mother Hosts, remarried

Mrs. Robert Wood
requests the honor of your presence
at the marriage of her daughter
Jaclyn Ann

### Bride's Mother and Stepfather Host

Mr. and Mrs. Michael Wood
request the honor of your presence
at the marriage of her daughter
Jaclyn Ann Dye

### Bride's Father Hosts
Mr. Joseph Dye
requests the honor of your presence
at the marriage of his daughter
Jaclyn Ann

### Bride's Father Hosts, remarried
Mr. and Mrs. Joseph Dye
request the honor of your presence
at the marriage of his daughter
Jaclyn Ann

### Bride's Divorced Parents Host
Mrs. Michael Wood
and
Mr. Joseph Dye
request the honor of your presence
at the marriage of their daughter
Jaclyn Ann Dye

### Second Marriage
Mr. and Mrs. Joseph Dye
request the honor of your presence
at the marriage of their daughter
Jaclyn Ann Dye Reese

### More Than Two Sets of Parents Host
Mr. and Mrs. Joseph Dye
Mr. and Mrs. Michael Wood
and
Mrs. and Mrs. Andrew Jones
request the honor of your presence
at the marriage of their children

### One Parent Deceased, Living Parent Not Remarried
Mrs. Joseph Dye
requests the honor of your presence
at the marriage of her daughter
Jaclyn Ann

### One Parent Deceased, Living Parent Remarried
Mr. and Mrs. Michael Wood
request the honor of your presence
at the marriage of her daughter
Jaclyn Ann Dye

### Close Relative Hosts
Mr. and Mrs. Paul Morgan
request the honor of your presence
at the marriage of their granddaughter
Jaclyn Ann Dye

 **Alert**

The name of a deceased parent is not included on the invitation. It shows no disrespect to the parent that has passed away, and it is a practical matter, as a deceased parent cannot issue an invitation. It can only come from the widowed spouse, a living person.

### Bride and Groom with Children
Jaclyn Ann Dye
and
Arthur James Jackson
together with their children
Julie C. Dye, Ryan D. Dye, and Elizabeth A. Jackson

## Military Protocol

**What is proper for a military wedding?** In military weddings, rank determines the placement of names. If the person's rank is lower than sergeant, omit the rank but list the branch of service of which the bride or groom is a member. Junior officers' titles are placed below their names and are followed by their branch of service. If the rank is higher than lieutenant, titles are placed before names and the branch of service is placed on the following line. Check with the specific branch's protocol officer if you have particular questions.

### Rank Lower Than Sergeant

Mr. and Mrs. Paul Parker
request the honor of your presence
at the marriage of their daughter
Renee Christine
United States Army
to
Kevin Avery Lee

### Junior Officers

Mr. and Mrs. Paul Parker
request the honor of your presence
at the marriage of their daughter
Renee Christine
to
Kevin Avery Lee
First Lieutenant, United States Navy

### Rank Higher Than Lieutenant

Mr. and Mrs. Paul Parker
request the honor of your presence
at the marriage of their daughter
Renee Christine

to
Captain Kevin Avery Lee
United States Navy

# Please, Mr. Postman

You found the perfect invitation, you penned the perfect prose, and now your creation has arrived. Now what? At first, all the pieces of the invitation can seem like a puzzle, making the job of getting them in the mail seem like a daunting task. But fear not! A little organization combined with some helpful hints will get you on your way to the post office in no time.

## Invitation Basics

**How is the invitation assembled?** The invitation is stacked from largest piece on the bottom (usually the invitation) to smallest piece on top. Place all the inserts by descending size on top of the invitation and then place the invitation and inserts into the inner envelope face-in. Make sure the inner envelope already has the guests' names written on it. Finally, insert the inner envelope into the outer envelope so that the handwritten names face the back of the envelope.

**When should the invitations be sent out?** Mail the invitations approximately eight weeks before the wedding, with an R.S.V.P. date of about three weeks before the wedding. If you're planning a wedding near a holiday, mail out your invitations a few weeks earlier to give your guests some extra time to plan.

 **Alert**

Take one fully assembled invitation to the post office and have it weighed for correct postage. Most wedding invitations require extra postage, either for weight or for size regulations. The last thing you need is all of your beautiful invitations returned to you and stamped, "Returned for Insufficient Postage."

## Addressing the Issue

**My friends Andrew and Lisa are platonic roommates. Can I send one invitation to both of them?** Your friends should each get a separate invitation—whether or not they live together. The only instance in which you would send two friends the same invitation is if they are romantically involved, married, or living together.

**Do we need to send an invitation to our attendants?** Although a reply is not expected or required, you should send invitations to everybody involved in the wedding. This includes attendants, siblings, parents, and the officiant, along with their respective significant others. You don't need to send invitations to whoever is issuing the invitation.

**What is the proper way to address invitations?** Addressing the invitation properly depends on the circumstances. The following guidelines will assist you in sorting out any addressing issues:

**Professional titles:** The names should be written on one line; the person with the title is listed first.
*Outer:* Dr. Caroline Smith and Mr. Frederick Smith
*Inner:* Dr. and Mr. Smith

**If the couple are both medical doctors, the envelope should be addressed to:**
*Outer and inner:* The Doctors Smith

**An unmarried couple living together or a married couple with different last names:** Each person's full name should be on a separate line, with the woman's name listed first.
*Outer:* Ms. Kathy Smith
Mr. Neil Jones
*Inner:* Ms. Smith and Mr. Jones

**A married or unmarried same-sex couple using different last names:** List the names alphabetically.
*Outer:* Ms. Nancy Jones

Ms. Kathy Smith
*Inner:* Ms. Jones and Ms. Smith

**An entire family:** The parents' names are on the outer envelope, and their children's names are added to the inner envelope descending by age order.
*Outer:* Mr. and Mrs. John Smith
*Inner:* Mr. and Mrs. Smith
Jennifer, Joseph, and Jules

**A married same-sex couple with hyphenated last names:**
*Outer:* Mrs. and Mrs. Jennifer and Marie Jones-Smith
*Inner:* Mrs. and Mrs. Jones-Smith

**A married same-sex couple using one last name:**
*Outer:* Mrs. and Mrs. Jennifer and Marie Jones
*Inner:* Mrs. and Mrs. Jones

 **Essential**

If you are sending an invitation to a single woman who's been married before and she has elected to retain her married last name, use "Mrs." regardless of her present marital status. If she has decided to use her maiden name, Ms. would be appropriate. In recent years, many brides have elected to use "Miss" for those under eighteen and "Ms." for any ladies over eighteen.

**Are there any other etiquette rules I should know about when addressing the invitations?** There are a few more pointers for addressing the invitations. Never connect two names with "and" unless the two people are a married couple. If the names are too long to fit on one line, indent the second name under the name on the first line. Never put either "and guest" or "and family" on the invitation; the former is considered rude and impersonal, while the latter denotes the invitee's entire family.

# CHAPTER 10

# Getting to "I Do"

*A*re you finding yourself wondering, "Where and when does the 'I do' fit into this journey?" Well, rejoice! It is getting closer. Soon you will be making the transition from engaged to married, and while this is an exciting milestone, it can be a nerve-wracking experience too. Stay focused on the end result and create a meaningful ceremony that honors this rite of passage.

## Types of Ceremonies

The type of ceremony you select will have a lot to do with your religious upbringing. You also need to take into account your fiancé's views, not to mention your parents' belief system.

### Religious Ceremonies

**Must all religious weddings take place in a house of worship?** No, but it depends on your particular religion or wishes. Some officiants are willing to marry you in the location of your choice.

### Civil Ceremonies

**What is a civil ceremony?** Civil ceremonies are nonreligious and presided over by a civil or government official. Civil ceremonies can be as formal and dramatic as traditional church weddings, just without the limitations of religious laws or regulations. You will need a marriage license, and you may need witnesses; each state has different requirements.

## Nondenominational Ceremonies

**What is a nondenominational wedding ceremony?** This is a ceremony that emphasizes religion without being associated with any particular religion. It is often free of the structure and restrictions of traditional religious ceremonies but does have a religious tone.

 **Essential**

Nondenominational ceremonies are a popular choice for couples who do not have a strong religious background, have different religious backgrounds, are marrying in a place other than a house of worship, or want free rein to create their own ceremony.

## Interfaith Ceremonies

**What is an interfaith ceremony?** An interfaith marriage joins two people from different religions. Some religions will permit and recognize these unions, while some prohibit them and will not recognize the union.

**What are the rules regarding interfaith marriages?** Early in the planning, make it a high priority to consult with both sets of clergy to get a clear picture of what rules and restrictions each religion, clergy, and house of worship has on the matter. Some will happily accept this union, others will have stipulations, and there are some that will not allow this at all.

In general, the Catholic Church will sanction a marriage between a Catholic and non-Catholic providing that all of the

Church's concerns are met. In marriages between a Protestant and a Catholic, officiants from both religions may take part in the ceremony if the couple wishes, and arrangements are made in advance. Quakers, Hindus, and Buddhists, to name a few, are more open and accepting of interfaith marriages. The Church of Latter Day Saints, Reform Judaism, and Islam will also tolerate these unions. On the bright side of all of this, there are (for-hire) officiants representing all denominations, and they are usually more flexible with their terms of services. Now you may not be able to marry in a house of worship, but you just might be able to have officiants from both faiths freely perform the ceremony at a neutral or agreed-upon location.

## Commitment Ceremonies

**What is a commitment ceremony?** When two people chose to not be married legally (for whatever reasons) or cannot be married legally (for example same-sex couples in certain states), they may choose to celebrate their union with a commitment ceremony. The commitment ceremony can have all the same traditions and grandeur as any other ceremony, as well as be overseen by a religious officiant (if the couple chooses). The main difference between a commitment ceremony and other types of ceremonies is that the commitment ceremony has no legality.

## Rules and Rituals of Marriage

Each religion and each house of worship reserves a special set of rules, requirements, and rituals for marriage. When you are working with your officiant, be sure to discuss these rules and make sure you really understand their significance. While the rules cover everything from photography to dress, the rituals are generally what distinguish the different religions and ceremonies from one another.

## Religious Requirements

**What are the requirements to marry in the Roman Catholic, Protestant, or Jewish faiths?** Religions differ too much to make one blanket statement. The following information should give you a general idea about what to expect:

- Roman Catholic couples must receive extensive Pre-Cana (pre-marriage) counseling, involving discussions with your priest about your religious convictions and important marriage issues, workshops with other engaged couples, and compatibility quizzes. Marriage Banns must be announced three times prior to the wedding date. If you've been married before in the Catholic Church, you must receive an annulment from the Church.

- Protestant marriages, regardless of denomination, have far fewer requirements and restrictions than Catholic marriages. One or more informal meetings with the minister are required. Premarital counseling, though less rigorous than Pre-Cana, is common. You may also need to take compatibility quizzes. Sunday weddings are generally discouraged. There is no need for an annulment if either party has been divorced.

- The Orthodox and Conservative branches of Judaism rigidly adhere to a few stipulations: Weddings may not take place on the Sabbath or during any other time that is considered holy, men must wear yarmulkes, and ceremonies are generally performed in Hebrew or Aramaic. Neither of these branches will conduct interfaith ceremonies. The Reform branch adheres to the same basic stipulations; however, some Reform rabbis will conduct interfaith ceremonies. In all cases, if either party is divorced, the couple is required to obtain a Jewish divorce, or get, before they can remarry.

## Military Rules and Tradition

**What defines a military wedding?** Military weddings are impressive and formal affairs. Either you or your fiancé need to be in the military in order to have a military wedding. Wedding guests and wedding party members who are members of the armed forces dress in uniform. Despite the differences in attire and protocol, a military wedding can be as much like a traditional wedding as you wish. There are also special military traditions you may like to include in your special day. In one, the newly married couple walks arm and arm from the altar beneath an archway of crossed swords. The bride and groom can also cut the first piece of their wedding cake with a sword.

**What is the proper attire for a military wedding?** A groom serving in the armed forces must wear his dress uniform in the ceremony. As part of his outfit he may wear a sword or saber but never a boutonnière. If the groom wears a sword, the bride stands on his right, away from the blade; if not, she stands on his left. A military bride has the choice of wearing her dress uniform or a traditional wedding gown. Other military personnel in the wedding party and wedding guests, male or female, usually wear a military uniform.

 **Alert**

The seating at a military wedding has to account for high-ranking officers and special officials. These people must be seated in places of honor. The bride or groom's commanding officer along with his spouse may be seated in the front row on the respective side if the parents are not present. Or, he and his spouse may sit in the second or third row with the family. The remainder of the military guests should be seated by rank in the rows just behind the family.

# The Officiant

Finding just the right person to marry you is a crucial decision. The type of service and the way it is performed can make the ceremony that much more meaningful. If you regularly attend a house of worship or plan to marry in a house of worship, your first inquiry should be there. If you are marrying elsewhere, you have many options for finding just the right officiant to perform your service.

## Finding an Officiant

**If I am not marrying in a house of worship, how do I find an officiant?** You can find an officiant who will marry you in the location of your choosing quite easily. Just as when you look to hire other vendors, consult friends, a wedding planner, the Internet, or a local bridal magazine/guide for leads on officiants. If you attend a house of worship, you can ask that officiant if he will perform the ceremony elsewhere; he may or may not, depending on religious requirements.

## Working with an Officiant

**How much do I pay or tip my officiant?** If you are marrying in a house of worship, there is typically a donation involved and other set fees for services, such as those of the venue coordinator, musicians, and other personnel related to the venue. If you are hiring an officiant, the fees will vary based on a number of factors, including location and type of service.

## Questions to Ask the Officiant

**How do I know if I am hiring the right officiant?** Ask the officiant some important questions to determine if this person is right for your wedding.

- Is premarital counseling required?
- How do you charge for your services? Do you require a deposit to hold the date?
- Do you have sample ceremonies we can work from?
- How much personalization is allowed in the ceremony?
- May we write our own vows?
- What restrictions are there on photography or videography during the ceremony?
- How long do your ceremonies typically last?
- Are readings or solos allowed?
- Will participation from another clergy be allowed?
- What is your attire on the wedding day?
- Are there any other rules we should know about?
- Are you available for the rehearsal? If so, will you assist in conducting the rehearsal?
- What is the cost for the use of the facility? Does this include the coordinator?
- What is available to use in terms of aisle runners, altar/pew decorations, and musical talent?
- What is the policy for bringing in our own musicians?
- Will a receiving line be allowed at the facility?
- Are there other events scheduled for that day? If so, how much time will we have for setting up and decorating?

 **Essential**

If you are marrying in a house of worship, you will most likely be working with the site coordinator. This person, often a volunteer, has typically overseen numerous weddings and events at her particular location and knows it inside and out. She should be able to answer your questions and concerns and provide you with guidance.

## Licenses and Legalities

Plan all you want, but if you forget this one important detail, it is all for nothing. The marriage license is the official document that makes your union legal. You can obtain one through a simple process that can be done quickly at the county clerk's office, city hall, or even a specialized service that comes to you.

**How do we get a marriage license?** To get your marriage license, in most cases you and your fiancé will need to apply together, in person. You will both need to be of legal age or have the written consent of your guardians. Additional requirements vary by state, but generally you will need a valid identification (such as a driver's license or military identification), proof of divorce or dissolution if either of you has been married before, and money to pay the license fee.

**Is there a waiting period?** In some states there is a waiting period from the time you apply for your license until the time you can get married. Be sure to check on these requirements early on in the planning, especially if you live in a different state from the one in which you will be married. Additionally, a marriage license is only valid for a set amount of time, so don't get the license too early.

## Global Customs

Taking a closer look at your own heritage as well as some global wedding traditions may inspire ideas for your wedding ceremony.

### Celebrate Your Heritage

**I want to incorporate traditions from my heritage. Where do I begin?** Find inspiration by talking to your parents or grandparents. Have your fiancé do the same and then see which pieces

of your past you would like to include. Once you find the traditions or rituals you like, look to incorporate a few here and there.
If possible, be sure to include the reason and description of these
rituals in the wedding program so the guests understand what
and why they are included.

## Culture Cues

**I would like to include some more worldly elements into
my wedding. Where do I start?** First try to "borrow" elements
from your heritage and your fiancé's heritage. If that is not giving you enough inspiration or if you and your fiancé do not have
strong cultural ties, seek inspiration from a culture you admire or
a country you have traveled to and have a particular interest in.

 **Alert**

> Certain traditions and rituals are closely associated with par-
> ticular religions or cultures, and a literal translation of the
> custom into your ceremony may not be quite right; in fact, it
> could even offend some. Be creative, but be sensitive when
> incorporating "new" elements into your ceremony.

**What are some simple ideas from other cultures that I can
incorporate into my wedding?** There are many ways to incorporate a global perspective into your wedding. Here are a couple
of ideas that can easily be incorporated into many weddings:
- For the Jewish custom of Yichud, the bride and groom are
  immediately escorted to a private room after the ceremony,
  where they spend some time alone. You too can sneak
  away to spend a few moments with your new spouse before
  hitting the reception. Ask the caterer to have champagne
  and hors d'oeuvres waiting for you.

- The Chinese tea ceremony is traditionally the final duty of the bride on her wedding day. In a special room with a table complete with symbolic offerings, the bride serves tea to the groom's family, beginning with the oldest and continuing until she reaches the youngest member. Upon finishing the tea, the bride takes the cup and in turn is presented with a monetary gift in a red envelope. You can incorporate this Chinese tradition by inviting your parents and your husband's parents to join you in a separate room or private area for a special toast that can be done with tea, champagne, wine, water, or a specialty beverage.

# CHAPTER 11

# I Now Pronounce You

*Y*ou walk down the aisle, say "I do," and walk out a married couple. The glorious event that will unite you and your fiancé is over and you can now live happily ever after. Sounds simple, right? Well, there is a lot more to it than that. Saying your "I dos" is a life-changing event, and too often couples focus on the wedding and not on the marriage. Spend some time creating a beautiful and memorable ceremony to mark the beginning of your married life.

## Planning the Ceremony

Once you have determined where you will be marrying, who will be marrying you, and the type of service, it is time to plan the ceremony itself. Incorporating traditions and adding a touch of personalization are important aspects to planning an unforgettable ceremony.

### Deciphering the Ceremony

**What does a Roman Catholic ceremony generally entail?**
The Roman Catholic wedding ceremony consists of Introductory Rites, including opening music selections, a greeting by the priest, and an opening prayer; Liturgy of the Word, including readings by your friends and family members and a homily that focuses on some aspect of marriage; and the Rite of Marriage, including the declaration of consent and the exchange of vows and rings.

Having a complete Mass is optional; with it, the ceremony will typically last 45 minutes.

**What does a Jewish ceremony generally entail?** Judaism has different branches that adhere to different rules, but certain elements of the wedding ceremony are basically the same. In the Orthodox, Conservative, and Reform traditions, both sets of parents are part of the ceremony and escort their children down the aisle, wine is shared from a kiddush cup, a ketubah is signed, the couple is married under a chuppah, and a rabbi presides over the ceremony. There are additional portions of the ceremony that vary based upon the type of Judaism the couple observes.

**What is generally included in a Protestant ceremony?** The Protestant wedding ceremony varies somewhat among the denominations, but the basic elements are the same. The officiant welcomes the guests, and a Prayer of Blessing is said. Scripture passages are read, there is a Giving in Marriage (affirmation by parents), and the congregation gives its response. After vows and rings are exchanged, there is a celebration of the Lord's Supper, and the unity candle is lit, followed by the Benediction and recessional.

## Special Elements

**What is a reading?** Readings are poems, passages, or scriptures that focus on some aspect of togetherness and marriage. They are read during the ceremony by a special friend, relative, or even a member of the bridal party. If you select your own readings, be sure to get approval from your officiant.

**What symbolic ceremonies can I include?** Symbolic ceremonies emphasize togetherness and the joining of families. One of the most popular ceremonies is the lighting of the unity candle. The sand ceremony, wine ceremony, and rose ceremony are other options. In a sand ceremony, the bride and groom simultaneously fill one vessel from two others filled with sand. In a wine ceremony, the bride and groom each sip from a single glass of wine. In a rose ceremony, the bride and groom present the other's mother with a rose. Of course, be sure to consult with your officiant regarding specific details and possible restrictions.

 **Fact**

> The unity candle represents the joining of two families. During the ceremony, the mothers come forth and light two candles representing each family. Later in the ceremony, the bride and groom will be asked to use these candles and, together, light one candle representing the two becoming one.

## Vows

**Should we write our own vows?** Writing your own vows is a personal choice, and you must be comfortable expressing yourself and sharing your feelings before a roomful of people. If you don't feel quite comfortable with that but would still like to personalize your vows, include a poem or passage that complements the vows. Be sure to discuss this with your officiant, as some religions have strict rules about what vows must be said.

## Sample Ceremony Outline

**Is there a typical format for a ceremony?** Most wedding ceremonies follow a similar outline. They will all differ slightly depending on your officiant and religious affiliation. There are many ways to customize a ceremony by including readings, musical selections, and symbolic ceremonies. The following are the basic components of a wedding ceremony:

- **Prelude:** The thirty minutes prior to the ceremony when guests arrive and are seated.

- **Processional:** Signals the beginning of the ceremony. This is when the parents are seated and the groom, best man, and officiant take their places, followed by the entrance of the wedding party and bride.
- **Welcome:** The officiant welcomes the guests.
- **Giving Away or Recognition of the Parents:** The officiant asks some version of "who gives this woman to marry this man?"
- **Charge to the Couple:** The officiant confirms each party has come to marry of their own free will.
- **Exchange of Vows:** The couple recites their vows to one another.
- **Ring Ceremony:** The bride and groom will each give and receive a wedding ring.
- **Pronouncement:** The officiant proclaims you are officially and legally married.
- **Recessional:** The official exit from the church as a married couple. You and your husband will lead the recessional, followed by pairs of the bridal party.

 Essential

To emphasize the role of both parents leading their children through life, and to demonstrate the uniting of the families, both parents escort their children down the aisle in a Jewish processional. Even if you are not Jewish, you may take a cue from this ritual and invite both of your parents to walk you down the aisle, too.

## Get Me to the Church on Time

Have you thought about how and when will you arrive at the ceremony? How will you keep the groom from catching a glimpse of you? Make a plan; these important logistical decisions are all too often overlooked until the last minute.

## Getting Ready

**Can I get ready at the church?** Most houses of worship don't allow you to get ready on the premises, mainly because of time and space restrictions. They will often allow the bride to put her gown on at the location. You should plan on arriving with your hair and makeup done so you can easily slip on the gown. The bridesmaids, groomsmen, and families should be completely ready.

**When should I arrive for the ceremony?** Every location is different, but plan on arriving about sixty to ninety minutes prior to the ceremony start time. This should be enough time to slip into your gown, take a few photos, and slip away before the guests begin arriving.

## To See or Not to See

**Can my fiancé and I take photos together prior to the ceremony?** The tradition that dictated the bride and groom should not see each other before the ceremony is a thing of the past. Today it's perfectly acceptable for the happy couple to lay eyes on each other before they say "I do." This gives a nervous couple a moment together, and it's also an opportunity to take photos. Though this is a popular and common practice, many traditionalists still frown on it.

## Ceremony Seating

Not only do you need to figure out how to get everyone down the aisle, but you must also figure out where everyone is going to sit. There are places of honor to consider, as well as divorces and remarriages to take into account.

## Pick a Side, Any Side

**Which side of the aisle is appropriate for the bride's family?** The bride's family traditionally sits on the left side of the church for a Christian ceremony, while the groom's family sits on the right. The reverse is true for Reform and Conservative Jewish weddings. However, men and women are usually segregated in Orthodox Jewish weddings.

 **Fact**

Guests are seated as they arrive, from front to back. The mothers of the bride and groom should be seated just before the ceremony begins. Sometimes the grandparents are seated just prior to the mothers. Late-arriving guests are usually asked to wait until the bride has walked down the aisle.

**What does "within the ribbons" mean?** In some ceremonies, the first few rows of pews or chairs are sectioned off by ribbons, meaning they are reserved for family and very special friends. It is not necessary to provide this kind of seating, but if you do, include "within the ribbons" cards with the guest's invitation. The guests should bring this card and present it to the ushers so that they can be seated appropriately.

## Family Distractions

**My parents are divorced. Where should they be seated during the ceremony?** Typically, parents are seated in the first row (or in the second if the attendants will be seated during the ceremony). In the case of divorce, the bride's natural mother has the privilege of sitting in the first row and of selecting those who will sit with her, including her spouse if she has remarried. If your divorced parents have remained amicable, your father may sit in the second row with his spouse or significant other. He may also sit in the front row if all parties agree to it. If there is some acrimony between the two parties, however, your father should be seated a few rows farther back. However, if you have been raised by your stepmother and prefer to give her the honor, she and your father may sit in the first row, while your mother sits farther back.

**Where should my siblings and grandparents be seated during the ceremony?** Your siblings should sit in the second row, behind your mother and father. Grandparents sit in the third row, and close friends and relatives sit in the fourth.

## The Processional

The walk down the aisle is one of the most important and memorable walks of your life. Before you get to take the walk, a few other important people need to precede you. Getting all of the important members of the family and wedding party to their places is the purpose of the processional.

### Walking Down the Aisle

**In what order do attendants walk down the aisle in Christian ceremonies?** In a Catholic processional, the bridesmaids walk down the aisle one by one, while the groomsmen and best man wait at the altar. Who goes first is usually determined by height, from shortest to tallest. For large weddings with more than four bridesmaids, they walk in pairs. The honor attendant is next, followed by the ring bearer and flower girl. The bride then enters on her father's right arm, followed by pages (if any), who carry the bride's train. The Protestant processional is the same, except ushers may precede the bridesmaids in pairs, according to height.

**In what order do attendants walk down the aisle in Jewish ceremonies?** Orthodox, Conservative, and Reform processions vary according to the families' preferences, devoutness, and local custom. A traditional religious Jewish processional may begin with the rabbi and cantor (with the cantor on the rabbi's right), followed by the ushers walking one by one, and the best man. The groom then walks between his mother on his right and his father on his left. The bridesmaids then walk one by one, followed by the maid of honor, the page, and the flower girl. The bride is the last to enter, with her mother on her right and her father on her left.

## Giving the Bride Away

**My parents are divorced and my mother has remarried. Is it more appropriate for my father or my stepfather to walk me down the aisle?** This really depends on who raised you, your personal preference, and your current family situation. If you've remained close to your father, you may prefer that he fulfill his traditional role. If both men have been involved in your life, consider including both men in the proceedings. For example, have both men escort you down the aisle, or have one escort you halfway down the aisle until you meet up with the other, who will finish the walk with you. In Jewish ceremonies, divorced parents both walk the bride down the aisle.

**My father has passed away. Who should escort me down the aisle?** There is really no single correct answer. When considering your options, what is most important is that you do whatever feels most comfortable to you. Some brides walk down the aisle with their mother or even with their groom. If your mother has remarried and you are close to your stepfather, he may be a good choice. A brother, grandfather, special uncle, or close family friend could also do the honors. Of course, there is always the option to walk without an escort. Keep in mind that whomever you choose should sit in the front pew with your mother during the ceremony (except if you choose your groom, of course).

 **Essential**

If the tradition of the father giving the bride away is too old-fashioned, there are alternatives. Instead of the officiant asking "Who gives this woman . . . ?" he may ask, "Who blesses this union?"

## Double Take

**In a double wedding, do the brides walk down the aisle together? If not, how do we decide who goes first?** The undisputed law of etiquette is clear: the older of the two brides is the first to perform all key wedding rites, and so she is the one who processes down the aisle first with her wedding party. However, aside from the fact that everything is done twice, the double wedding can be just like any other wedding.

## The Recessional

The recessional, your first walk as a married couple, signifies the beginning of your new life. After months and months of planning, you are finally married, and it is time to celebrate. As the guests rise and applaud your joyous exit, take a minute to bask in the glow of being a newlywed.

**What is the appropriate order of the recessional?** Arm in arm, you and your new husband (yes, finally, your husband!) lead the recessional, followed by your child attendants. Your maid of honor and best man are next, followed by your bridesmaids, who are paired with ushers. The order of the Jewish recession is as follows: bride and groom, bride's parents, groom's parents, child attendants, honor attendants, and bridesmaids paired with ushers. The cantor and rabbi follow.

# CHAPTER 12

# Greeting the Guests

*T*hey're coming! They're coming! Yes, the guests are finally coming. Now what are you going to do with them? Having people come from all over to attend your wedding is an honor, and you should make it a smooth journey for them by providing travel information, activities to entertain, and a warm welcome to greet them upon their arrival. Don't forget about planning the wedding rehearsal and the rehearsal dinner!

## The Rehearsal

You want everything to flow smoothly on your wedding day, and a well-orchestrated rehearsal is the key to success. Usually the night before the wedding, you will gather all involved parties at the ceremony site so they can familiarize themselves with the venue and participate in a quick run-through of the ceremony. Afterward, it is off to a fun and relaxing evening with friends and family at the rehearsal dinner.

### Why a Rehearsal?

**What is the rehearsal for?** The rehearsal shows everyone involved what to do, where to go, and when to do it. It prepares the wedding party and families for the events of the wedding day and gives them a chance to acquaint themselves with the location.

## Planning the Rehearsal

**What can I expect at the rehearsal?** The officiant or wedding planner will go over rules and special information and do a quick run-through of the ceremony from processional to recessional, making sure that the wedding party and parents know their positions/seats, ushers learn their duties, readers practice their readings, and soloists run through their pieces.

 **Alert**

If you hired an officiant, be sure to ask if he will be attending the rehearsal. You should also clarify if this is included in his fee or if there is an additional charge. If the officiant attends the rehearsal, he and his spouse should be invited to the rehearsal dinner.

**Who runs the wedding rehearsal?** At a house of worship, their wedding coordinator usually runs the rehearsal. At other venues, you or your wedding planner will run the rehearsal; not all hired officiants attend the rehearsal. If you will be in charge, work things out very clearly with your officiant, including how the processional and recessional should be orchestrated. Plan out how you want everyone to enter and where they will stand, as well as where you want the parents to be seated. If possible, enlist the help of a friend who is not in the wedding party to assist at the rehearsal. Or better yet, look into hiring a wedding planner to run the rehearsal and the ceremony on the wedding day.

## The Rehearsal Dinner

The rehearsal dinner is a time for the people involved in the wedding to gather and enjoy some special, more intimate time together prior to the big day. The rehearsal dinner is the time for personal stories, reminiscing, and toasts. It is also a good opportunity for the bride and groom to express their gratitude to the family and wedding party.

## Who's Invited?

**Do I have to invite all of the out-of-town guests to my rehearsal dinner?** If money and space permit, inviting the out-of-town guests is a nice gesture, but it is not required. Strictly speaking, the following people should be invited: immediate families of the couple (parents, siblings, and grandparents), the wedding party and their spouses/significant others (not dates) and their children (if they have traveled to attend the wedding), any children in the wedding party and their parents (depending on the time of the dinner), and the officiant and his spouse.

## What's It For?

**Do we need to have a rehearsal dinner?** Technically you do not need to have a rehearsal dinner, but it is expected and customary. The atmosphere is typically more relaxed and intimate than the wedding, and therefore it is a perfect time for personal toasts from the bride and groom, wedding party, and parents. A rehearsal dinner need not be a dinner either; it can be a brunch or lunch, whatever coincides best with the rehearsal time.

**Are there any traditions that should be followed at the dinner?** There is nothing that is required at the rehearsal dinner. Many times the couple will present the attendants and their parents with thank you gifts. Often there is a round of toasts, beginning with the groom toasting his bride and future in-laws, and then the bride toasting her groom and future in-laws. Sometimes the couple's parents like to get in a few words as well. Feel free to have as many toasts as you'd like; if everyone wants to make a toast and the mood calls for it, let them!

## Who Pays?

**Who pays for the rehearsal dinner?** Traditionally the groom's parents have the honor and expense of hosting the rehearsal dinner. However, it is not a faux pas for the bride's parents to throw the dinner if for some reason the groom's parents cannot. The bride's parents, and even you and your fiancé, can pitch in for the dinner. Of course, the hosts should consult the bride and groom about locations and other details.

**Do we need to send formal invitations for the rehearsal dinner?** A phone call can suffice as an invitation, but sending a printed invitation is perfectly fine. The invitations need not be formal, and can simply be purchased at the local stationery store or printed on the computer.

**My fiancé's mother thinks she doesn't need to pay for our guests' drinks at the rehearsal dinner. Is she right?** The guests shouldn't be expected to pay for anything. Enough said.

## Transportation Conundrums

As a courteous host, providing travel and hotel information to the guests will make their journey to your wedding a smooth and enjoyable one. An itinerary of the wedding activities lets the guests know what to expect, and a small hospitality package will provide a warm welcome after a long trip.

**Do I need to pay for the guests' travel arrangements?** You are not required to pay for any portion of the guests' travel arrangements. As an acceptance of your invitation, they assume the responsibility of paying their own way to your wedding. Of course, if your financial situation can accommodate such arrangements, it is perfectly okay to do so.

146

 **Fact**

Group airfare discounts will provide some welcome economic relief for guests that will be flying in to attend your wedding. Generally, the airlines ask that a minimum number of fares be purchased from them in exchange for a discount. Check out the airline's website or call them directly to find out their requirements. Car rental agencies may also offer special group discounts for weddings.

**My wedding location is a little off the beaten path. Should I provide transportation to and from the ceremony and reception?** Providing transportation is not necessary (and is an additional expense), but guests would surely appreciate the hospitality of shuttle buses or luxury coaches to take them to the wedding festivities. You should designate times and meeting locations at the guests' hotels and provide the guests with a timeline for arrivals and departures. Such arrangements ensure your guests get to the ceremony and reception on time, and no one will have to worry about driving if they have a little champagne.

## A Warm Welcome

Guests who attend your wedding are making an effort to be there to witness this cherished moment in your life. After traveling, there is nothing more wonderful than arriving at your destination and being welcomed with open arms. Take care to provide the guests with a list of activities and some genuine hospitality to make this a wedding and a trip they will never forget.

**What is a hospitality basket or package?** A hospitality package is a welcome gift of travel amenities and/or snacks from the bride and groom to the guests. You will need one package per room, but be sure to include the appropriate number of items, such as water bottles to accommodate the number of guests in the room. These are not necessary, but guests appreciate them and they make a great impression.

**What should I include in the hospitality package?** The packages can be as simple as bottled water and snacks (cookies, gum or mints, nuts, crackers, chocolates, trail mix, dried fruit, fresh fruit), or they can be more elaborate and include gourmet food selections and wine. Your packages can be created to reflect your wedding destination or theme as well—for example, a bottle of wine for a wine country wedding or beach towels for a beachfront destination. A welcome letter, wedding activities guide or itinerary, and a local travel guide are also great additions.

## The Party Begins . . . The Party Continues

In addition to the excitement of the wedding itself, there are a few other wedding activities you may want to plan for your guests. While it is not your responsibility to plan out each minute of the guest's stay, the addition of pre- and post-wedding parties will surely be enjoyed and welcomed.

### Pre-Parties

**I cannot invite everyone to the rehearsal dinner but feel bad about excluding guests, especially those who have traveled so far. Any ideas?** Ask a close friend or relative if they would be willing to host an informal cocktail party at their home, or plan to have everyone meet up at the hotel, restaurant, or bar for a drink after the rehearsal dinner. Plan this carefully because you should attend any events you invite guests to, at least for a short while. Depending on the circumstances, you should also host the activity. You should include a line such as "Be our guest at the hotel bar for a pre-wedding party. Hosted from 8:00 P.M. to 9:30 P.M."

## Post-Parties

**We would like to have a post-reception party at a local bar. Must we host the event or can we have a no-host event?** Once you have treated the guests to a fine celebration complete with food and drink, this is one activity you need not host. Just be sure to let the guests in on this detail via the welcome letter, the wedding website, and by word of mouth.

**Do we need to host a brunch on the day after the wedding?** Brunches have become common and are customary in certain regions but are by no means mandatory. The brunch doesn't have to be extravagant; a Continental breakfast with juices, coffee, and pastries will suffice. You should extend this invitation to the out-of-town guests, and you may include locals as well.

# Thank You for Coming

The receiving line gets a fair amount of bad press, mainly because couples are not quite sure what it entails or what to do. They can only envision a long line of anxious guests waiting . . . and waiting. As a result, it's usually the first thing to get axed. However, with proper protocol and a plan, the receiving line can be a lot of fun for you and it is a great way to connect with the guests.

**What is a receiving line?** The receiving line enables you, your groom, your parents, and key members of the wedding party to meet and greet your guests. The order from the head of the line is: bride's mother, bride's father, groom's mother, groom's father, bride, groom, maid of honor, and bridesmaids. Traditionally, the inclusion of the fathers in the receiving line is optional, but many fathers choose to participate. Additionally, while the maid of honor is a part of the receiving line, the best man does not usually join in.

**We're having a rather large wedding. How can we speed up the receiving line?** Keeping the line small; Including only the parents, you, and your husband, speeds up the process, keeping your greetings short and sweet helps too.

**Other than a receiving line, what else can we do to ensure that all our guests feel welcome?** Skipping the receiving line is fine, but it is imperative that you greet your guests and make them feel welcomed. Provided it doesn't interfere with serving the meal, go table to table to greet the guests throughout the event. Continue between courses, during the meal, and if necessary, as the dancing begins.

# CHAPTER 13

# The Celebration

*M*any brides feel pressured to have a large, formal reception because they think their guests expect it or, more often than not, because it is what they think a wedding reception is supposed to be. The truth is, the guests just want to celebrate with you, and a reception can be just about anything you want it to be. Plan a party that you are comfortable with, and when the day comes, relax and enjoy the fruits of your labor with your "old" family, your "new" family, and your friends.

## Planning the Reception

The wedding reception is most likely the biggest and most expensive party you will ever plan. It is the ultimate celebration of a glorious event in your life. Deciding between an informal cocktail hour or a plated dinner is only part of the story; there is more to the reception than just the meal.

### What Happens When

**What happens at the reception?** A wedding reception has three basic parts to it: cocktail hour, meal service, and dancing. The cocktail hour is the first item of business; guests arrive at the reception site and are greeted with hors d'oeuvres and refreshments, while the couple and wedding party finish up with their photos. At the conclusion of the cocktail hour, the guests are escorted into dinner for the grand entrance, the best man's toast, and the meal service. Once the meal is complete, dancing begins and the party really starts. More than likely there will be formal protocol dancing and then the guests will be invited to join in. The cake is cut and the bouquet and garter are tossed.

 **Alert**

Timing is everything. Delayed ceremonies beget delayed photography beget a delayed grand entrance beget a delayed meal. Not only will all of these delays upset the guests, but it will affect the quality of food and the flow or your reception.

## The Timeline

**What is a typical order of events at a wedding reception?**
There are many variations in timelines for modern weddings, all dependent upon individual circumstances. The following is a basic outline for the order of events at a reception. (For more information on the specifics of each tradition, see Chapter 15). You can work with your wedding planner, location manager, and musical entertainment to personalize your timeline.

**Reception Timeline**
- ❏ Cocktail hour
- ❏ Guests seated
- ❏ Grand entrance
- ❏ Welcome or blessing
- ❏ Best man's toast
- ❏ Meal service
- ❏ Additional toasts
- ❏ First dance
- ❏ Father/daughter dance
- ❏ Mother/son dance
- ❏ Wedding party dance

❑ Open dancing
❑ Cake cutting
❑ Bride and groom toast
❑ Garter and bouquet toss
❑ More dancing
❑ Send-off

## The Reception Venue

Throughout your planning, you will work with the venue's location manager to plan your meal, devise a floor plan, and finalize timing issues. A cooperative relationship with the location manager is a defining element of the reception. Much of the overall success of the wedding depends on the services of the reception venue and location manager.

### Expectations

**When I booked my reception venue, I saw a piano and some couches on-site. I recently asked to use them for my wedding and was told there would be additional charges. Is this fair?** Don't make assumptions about what your location will provide to you. Make sure you have in writing all the elements that you are expecting. Additionally, your contract should detail the times your venue is expecting you, including a time to access the room for setup, an invitation time, the hours of the event, the time the venue is expected to close, which rooms you have access to, and what food and beverages are being served. If the contract does not mention a dressing room, bring it up and make sure you can have access to a place you can change and store your wedding supplies and accessories.

**My wedding is in six months. Sometimes it takes more than twenty-four hours for my location to return my calls. I think I should expect faster service. Am I wrong?** Be aware that at any given time your location manages a great number of events. As other events approach their scheduled dates, they may demand more of the location manager's time and attention. As your own wedding date approaches, you, too, will receive the same attention. If your wedding is still six months out, a return call within twenty-four hours is still very good service.

## The Location Manager

**Who will be in charge of my wedding?** It works differently at all locations. Some venues have a location manager (sometimes called a catering or site manager) that will work closely with you on all details from the moment you book the location until you leave the reception as husband and wife. Other venues work with a more hands-off approach, assisting you with details related to the venue and nothing more. In many instances, the location manager is on-site for the beginning of your wedding to ensure everything is ready to go but may leave sometime after the reception begins, leaving you in the capable hands of the banquet captain.

 **Essential**

A location manager is not the same as a wedding planner. They each have different responsibilities, and one works for the venue and one works for you! If you do have a wedding planner, she will work with the catering manager to ensure your wedding runs smoothly.

## Questions to Ask

**What are some important questions to ask the location manager?** When you do visit locations, you should bring a list of questions to ask the location manager. Most of the questions, including those pertaining to meal service and pricing, will be answered during the meeting and tour or included in the information you receive at the meeting. Because you are touring and visiting multiple venues at first, it will be easy to forget what each location includes, requires, and costs, so take careful notes. Your questions will evolve to include more specifics once you book a venue and get closer to the wedding date. In general, the following questions apply to most locations:

- How many people can the area comfortably accommodate?
- How big is the dance floor?
- Are tables, chairs, dinnerware, silverware, and linens included in the price? Can we upgrade and what are those costs?
- How many hours is the site available? Can we book additional time? If so, at what cost? Are there overtime charges?
- Do you have a bride's room or a changing room?
- Can you accommodate special menu requests such as vegan or kosher meals?
- Will there be coatroom or restroom attendants?
- Do we need to hire security? Is it included in the price? If not, what is the cost?
- Will the location manager be able to assist me with creating a floor plan and décor?
- What is the parking situation? Is valet parking an additional cost? Is self-parking included? If not, how much does it cost?
- Are there any restrictions on musical entertainment?
- What are the restrictions on décor?
- If we purchase our own alcohol, is there a corkage fee?
- How many events can you accommodate at one time? Will there be an event taking place at the same time as my event? Before? After? Are there separate entrances, restrooms, and other facilities?

- Is there an area to hold the ceremony? Is there an additional charge?
- What do you require to book the location?
- What are your cancellation policies?

## Grilling the Caterer

Depending on your location, you may or may not have to hire an outside caterer. If you select a hotel or another wedding venue, they typically cater the meals themselves; however, if you select on offsite venue, you will need to hire a caterer. No matter what type of caterer you work with, there are a number of key questions you should ask before making a commitment. Once you've found a caterer with all the right answers, make sure to get every part of your agreement in writing.

 **Alert**

If you are hiring an outside caterer, you must make sure they have the proper amount of liability insurance to cover property damage, bodily injury, and accidents that could occur during and after the wedding as a result of alcohol being served. Most venues require this and will not let the caterer work at the site without it.

### Questions to Ask

**What questions should I ask the caterer?** Your questions will evolve to include more specifics once you book a venue and begin planning your menu. In general, the following questions apply to most caterers:

- What is the final food price?
- What types of meal service are offered?

- What are my menu options? Do you have predetermined menus or may I create my own?
- Do you provide bar service?
- Is the catering service covered with proper insurance?
- What will the ratio of staff to guests be? Will there be enough people to man the tables? Will those people be dressed appropriately for the occasion?
- Will they make provisions for guests with special dietary needs?
- Will meals be provided for the disc jockey or band, photographer, and videographer? What do you serve them and at what cost?
- What is the price difference between tray-passed hors d'oeuvres and a stationary display?
- Can you provide a wedding cake or other dessert?
- Is there a cake-cutting fee?
- Can you inspect rental items (linens, dinnerware, glassware, etc.)? Will you unpack and repack them for the rental company?
- Does the caterer's fee include gratuities for the staff? If not, what is customary? What is the fee for coatroom attendants, bartenders, and others who may be working at the reception?
- What is the cancellation and refund policy?
- What does the caterer do with leftover food?
- Do you have references?

 **Fact**

Weddings typically have a lot of leftover food, cake, and desserts. Contact a local food bank or shelter to see if they accept donations of your leftover reception food. There are strict regulations for this and transportation must be prearranged. Inquire early on to see if this is a possibility for your event.

# The Menu

The menu you select for the wedding meal should reflect the time of day and formality of the event. Would you serve BBQ ribs when your invitation asked for black-tie dress? When it is time to plan the menu, you must consider all of the elements of the wedding to make the right selections.

## Service Options

**What is the difference between buffet, sit-down, family style, or stations?** When it comes to meal service, you have options; however, you must realize particular venues and caterers may specialize in one style or another, and not all caterers and locations will be able to accommodate all of the options.

- The sit-down or plated meal is a traditional and usually more formal meal service. It usually involves at least three courses, a salad/soup/appetizer, an entrée, and a dessert. Other combinations include a salad/soup/appetizer, an intermezzo, and an entrée. Of course, many upscale locations offer four- and five-course meals as well.

- A buffet offers a display of food that guests can revisit as often as they like. For buffets, make sure there are enough clean plates for multiple visits through the line, that the catering manager or emcee of the evening has a system for sending guests to the buffet to avoid long lines, and finally, if it is a large wedding, that there are two or more buffet lines to avoid bottlenecking.

- Food stations offer a selection of made-to-order dishes. You can generally expect to have at least three stations set up around the venue, each offering specialties (sushi, pasta, salad, carving, etc.). Due to the labor involved (chefs on hand at each of the stations) this is one of the more costly options.

- Family-style meals are now being seen at both formal and at casual weddings. The caterer serves dishes to the tables and the guests pass them around, serving themselves as if they were in your home.

## What to Serve

**Our reception will begin at one o'clock and be over by five o'clock. Do we need to serve a sit-down meal?** Hors d'oeuvres or other light fare would be absolutely appropriate. If your reception will take place during a typical meal time, the guests will expect to be served a full meal.

**We gave our guests a choice of entrees, but how will the caterer know what each guest wants?** You should discuss this with your caterer or location manager before you determine the system, but generally you will use the escort or place card to designate the meal choice. One of the simplest ways to do this is to have the back of the card or another card state the guest's meal choice. The guest can simply hand the card to the wait staff. Another way is to put a clipart image representing the entree somewhere on the card (e.g., a cow for beef, a chicken for chicken, etc.). You can also use a decorative accessory, like a ribbon or crystal, to accent the card, with the accessory designating the meal choice. Lastly, using different colored cards is an option. For example, if your wedding colors are moss green, chocolate brown, and tangerine, use each color to indicate a meal choice. Ultimately what is important is that the wait staff knows what to look for and the caterer has an accurate count of the selections.

## Spirits

Weddings are known for their joviality. For better or for worse, much of the time this includes alcohol. A champagne toast, wine with dinner, and sometimes even shots at the bar are usually part of the celebration. Consider your guest list and your budget and then take some time to determine the style of beverage and/or bar service you will offer your guests.

 **Alert**

Many couples believe that to cut bar costs, they should purchase the alcohol themselves because the prices will be better and unopened bottles can be returned to the store. However, many venues will not allow alcohol to be brought in, some charge corkage fees that negate the savings, and most stores will not accept returns unless you have a prearranged agreement.

## The Bar

**I know having a cash bar is a no-no. Do I have options for alcohol service?** There are options when it comes to serving or not serving alcohol. The following are some ideas that you can use to determine the style of bar service at your event:

- Host a soft bar, including nonalcoholic refreshments, beer, and wine.
- Host a full open bar for a limited amount of time and then switch to a hosted soft bar.
- Serve sparkling wine instead of champagne.
- Offer house brands of alcohol rather than premium brands.
- Skip the champagne for the toast and let guests toast with what they are already drinking.
- If you know your guests are not drinkers or you are having a weekday or morning wedding (when guests usually consume less alcohol), have a consumption bar rather than purchasing the site's bar package.
- Ask the wait staff to only refill the guests' glasses when asked, not to top off automatically. Also instruct them

to not clear glasses unless they are empty or have been abandoned.

- Host an open bar only for the first hour of the reception. This will get things off on the right foot and many brides feel this fulfills their responsibility. This is a popular trend, but strictly speaking it breaks the laws of etiquette.

**What is a corkage fee?** In some instances when you bring in your own alcohol, the location may charge a convenience fee for opening each bottle. Be aware that a corkage fee may also be subject to the tax and service.

## Dos and Don'ts

**We're having a luncheon reception. Can we serve alcohol that early?** Liquor can be served anytime but should be appropriate to the occasion and time of day. For a luncheon reception, a fully stocked bar is unnecessary; mimosas, champagne, Bloody Marys, or other light drinks would be more appropriate.

 Question

Do I have to serve alcohol?
Nowhere does it state that you must serve alcoholic beverages at a wedding. Just because someone expects something doesn't mean it is a necessity. You must simply provide the guests with refreshments, and nonalcoholic beverages are perfectly fine.

**If we do not serve alcohol at our wedding, what should we serve to make up for it?** Ask the caterer to create a signature nonalcoholic drink, have a juice bar, or serve tropical iced teas and sparkling juices. A gourmet coffee bar always makes the guests happy.

CHAPTER 14

# Places, Please

*I*magine a flurry of hungry wedding guests entering the reception but not knowing where to go, where to sit, or what to do. Worse yet, picture your grandmother scrambling for a table only to be seated with your hard-partying college roommates, your shyest single friend, or twenty kids playing duck-duck-goose. Now, doesn't that make you realize the importance of a proper seating arrangement?

## The Seating Plan

Trying to come up with a seating plan that pleases everyone seems like an impossible task, but rest assured it does all work out—eventually. Realize that no matter how hard you try, someone—your mother, your fiancé's mother, your cousin, even your fiancé—is bound to have an opinion. You may feel like giving up, but don't despair; it really is worth the effort.

### How to Do It

**Is a seating plan really necessary?** A seating plan falls just short of being considered a necessity, but it is a courtesy and a convenience. Guests, especially those who don't know many people, often feel uncomfortable without assigned seating. If you're planning a cocktail party or not serving a full meal, a seating plan isn't necessary, but you should still have enough tables and chairs to accommodate all of your guests.

**How do I develop a seating plan?** Once the responses have been received, these simple steps will help you with the seating plan. Keep in mind that it may take a couple of revisions to get it just right.

- Obtain a floor plan from the venue that outlines the layout of the room (dance floor, bar, guest book, gift table, etc.).
- Decide where the head table, parents, and any other persons of honor will be sitting.
- Know how many guest tables you need. A general rule is eight to ten guests per sixty-inch round table.
- Match guests by families, where you know them from, or similar interests, and place them at tables.

 **Essential**

Place guests with special circumstances within the room so as to best accommodate their particular needs. Chances are Grandma doesn't want to sit by the band's speakers and the kids' table shouldn't be next to the head table. You will also want to think about wheelchair accessibility.

## Escort Cards

**How can I let guests know where they'll be sitting?** The easiest way to indicate table assignments is to have escort cards situated near the reception room entrance. Guests pick up the escort card to find their table assignment. If you are only assigning guests to a table, they may then find any seat they wish at that table. If you would like to designate a place setting, you will also need place cards on the dining tables. You do not need place cards if you are not designating place settings. But you should use place cards at the head table if your entire wedding party will be joining you.

## Places of Honor

The head table is wherever the bride and groom sit, and is, understandably, the focus of the reception. It is usually front and center in the room, and near the dance floor. The table is situated to allow guests a perfect view of you and your groom. While the tradition of a head table is still quite popular, there are now many options for seating the bride and groom.

### The Bride and Groom

**Rather than sitting at a traditional head table, what are our options?** A very popular alternative is the sweetheart table, which is a table just for two. Many couples prefer this option because it lets them have a little time together to eat their meal and it also allows the attendants to sit with their spouses/significant others. You can also sit at a "regular" guest table with your families and/or wedding party.

### The Head Table

**Who should sit at the head table?** Traditionally, the bride and groom, bridesmaids, and groomsmen sit at the head table. The bride and groom sit in the middle, with the groom on the bride's left, the best man next to the bride and the maid of honor next to the groom. The ushers and bridesmaids then sit on alternating sides of the bride and groom. Child attendants should sit at a regular table with their parents.

**We're having a rather large wedding party. How should we handle the head table?** A large head table is fine for a large wedding. Sometimes, two rows of tables, with one on a riser directly behind the other, can accommodate a large wedding party. Otherwise, you and your groom can sit at a sweetheart table and let your wedding party sit with their spouses, or you could sit with your honor attendants at the head table and seat the rest of your attendants together at guest tables.

## The Families and Wedding Party

**If we have a sweetheart table, where does the wedding party sit?** Most of the time, the wedding party would sit at one or two guest tables designated for them. They could also sit with their spouses throughout the room. Sometimes, a long table is set up behind the sweetheart table and the wedding party can sit there.

**My mother believes that parents should sit at the head table with the bride and groom, but I only want the wedding party at the head table. Is my mother right?** The head table is usually reserved for the members of the wedding party; parents usually sit at separate tables with their families. There's no single correct seating arrangement for the parents, however. The bride and groom's parents can sit together, or each set of parents can host their own table with family and friends. The officiant and his spouse should be seated at one of the parents' tables.

# Modern Seating

Forget about long, formal stuffy head tables and rounds of eight to ten guests. These are modern times, and with modern times come modern solutions. Sometimes, when trying to make the most of your venue or theme, round tables just don't cut it. A little creativity will add some wow to the reception and make finding the perfect place fun!

## Beyond Round Tables

**What is a feasting table?** A feasting table is one long table created by placing or grouping multiple rectangular tables together. Guests sit on either side of the table, and the look and feel is more reminiscent of a grand dining table in a glorious home. Some brides choose this for the head table and seat the guests at the traditional round tables.

 **Fact**

> If you think feasting tables are the way to go for your wedding, consult with the location manager and/or caterer first. Sometimes there is simply not enough space to accommodate multiple feasting tables due to the configuration of the room. Additionally, you may have to rent additional tables and linens to pull this look off, therefore incurring additional costs.

## Totally Modern

**I want to do something unique and out of the ordinary. In fact, I would like my wedding to not look like a wedding at all. How can I seat the guests?** You really need to think about your venue, your guests, and your style of meal before trying something too different. Start by deciding if an unconventional seating arrangement of couches, loungers, and coffee tables suit the venue. Then try to use what the venue offers; convert window seats, ledges, and low walls into guest seating by throwing cushions on them and pulling a table up. You can also rent low tables and throw a rug and cushions on the floor; just be sure to sit the younger crowd in these seats. Remember, you can mix in standard dining tables with these arrangements to accommodate all of your guests and your meal service. For example, elderly guests are going to expect—and probably prefer—a dining table, and if you are serving a formal dinner, it will be better to have a traditional dining arrangement.

## Not-So-Musical Chairs

By this point, you have probably already realized that planning a wedding requires a little extra maneuvering if you have divorced parents. If you're lucky, either your parents get along or they have agreed to declare a truce for a day. If you're not so lucky, seating arrangements can be a bit tricky. But as always, these problems can usually be solved through communication and flexibility.

### Divorced Parents

**Where should we seat divorced parents?** Divorced parents should not be seated at the same table, no matter how well they get along. If you're having a parents' table, have the parent who raised you sit with your in-laws and the officiant and seat your other parent with his or her own family and friends. Or, you can seat each parent at his or her own table with family and friends.

### Guest Dilemmas

**Where should attendants' spouses sit?** They can sit at tables with the other guests. Spouses don't usually sit at the head table with their husbands or wives.

**We have one set of friends that can get a little rowdy and like to drink. Is there something we can do to ward off a drunken party?** Short of not inviting them, there is not a whole lot you can force upon them. As for where you are going to sit them, put their table/tables on the opposite side of the room from the bar, and don't place them front and center so that they won't be a spectacle if they do drink too much. Also, tell the bartender that no shots are to be served at your wedding.

**My dad has been married numerous times. His third wife (he's on number four) will be attending, and I would like to**

**seat her someplace "special" but do not want to offend my father or his new wife. Where can I seat her?** Don't seat her too close to your father's table, as this is his time to celebrate with his friends and family. Look at your floor plan and seat her and her guest someplace out of eye shot of your father.

## Seating the Kids

You've made the decision to invite kids to your wedding. Now you need to figure out where to seat them. Not only do you need a seating plan that provides comfort and flexibility for both the kids and their parents, you really need to figure out how to keep them happy during the reception.

### The Kids' Table

**Should I have a kids' table at the wedding?** If there will be enough children at the reception to fill a table, a kids' table is great way for both the kids and the parents to enjoy themselves. If there are only a couple of children, you may just want to keep them with their parents. Children age seven and older are typically old enough to eat dinner at a table with the other kids. Think about the placement of the kids' tables and where the parents' tables are. Consider grouping those guests with kids in one area of the venue and placing the kids' tables in that same area. You can also mix the kids up by ages so that some older children will be available to assist the younger children.

### Keep Them Happy

**What do I need to have to create a fun kids' table?** For a kids' table, you should provide age-appropriate entertainment. Activities such as crayons and coloring books, activity books, and word searches will entertain children of many different ages. If it is possible and space allows, go the extra mile and talk to the venue about setting up a table or two for the kids to play board games, do puzzles, or even work on simple crafts.

 **Essential**

Hire a professional babysitter to take care of the kids. This can be done either in the reception room, in a nearby meeting room, or at a hotel room where the kids can hang out, watch movies, eat pizza, and fall asleep while their parents enjoy the wedding celebration.

**Do the kids get the same meal as the adults?** Generally, the kids get a kid-friendly meal, which typically costs less than the adult meals. You can determine a cut-off age, such as sixteen and under, for those who are to get the kids meal.

## Seating the Vendors

You already know that you should feed the vendors, but where are they supposed to sit? And when are they supposed to eat? The vendors working for you at your wedding can be some of your greatest allies when it comes to reception perfection, so treat them kindly and give 'em a break!

### You Sat Where?

**At the last wedding I attended, the vendors sat in empty seats with the guests. Where should they sit?** Having the vendors sit with the guests is the least desirable option for both the vendors and the guests. It can make the guests feel like they were seated at a "B-list" table, and the vendor really could use a break from the action. A vendor table in the back of the room is perfectly fine. If there is space, the best-case scenario would be to have a table set up outside of the main dining area on an adjacent patio, in the foyer, or in a nearby meeting room.

## Dinner Time

**When do the vendors eat?** Discuss the schedule with the caterer to find the time for the vendors to be served their meal without disrupting the guests' meal service or the reception activities. This best time is usually during the guests' meal service. Try to allot at least thirty minutes in the timeline for the vendors to eat and take a break. Provide them with their meal and nonalcoholic beverages. Professional vendors know what it takes to perform well at their jobs and they will not disappoint you. Many work with assistants so that while one eats, the other can cover the activities.

# CHAPTER 15

# Traditions

*I*t's hard to imagine a wedding without the traditions—the first dance, toasts, cutting the cake, the bouquet toss. These mini-events within the big event are fun, memorable, and part of what makes a wedding a wedding. While most couples want to include and honor tradition, they are constantly looking for ways to make their wedding unique. Lucky for them, traditions are constantly evolving, providing the opportunity to make a wedding one-of-a-kind.

## Hello, Goodbye

The grand entrance is your moment to shine, to revel in the happy moment of being a newly married couple. Wow the guests with the grand entrance, but realize in a blink of an eye you will be bidding them adieu. Put some serious thought into creating a one-of-a-kind entrance and exit that your guests will always remember.

### Grand Entrance

**What is the grand entrance?** The grand entrance is the first introduction of the bride and groom at the reception. This is generally the first order of business once the guests are in their seats. Traditionally the bride and groom and the entire wedding party are formally announced into the reception. Some couples choose to introduce only the bride and groom.

**How should we be introduced at the reception?** You have to take into account the formality of the wedding and what you feel comfortable with. "Mr. and Mrs. Joseph Mann" or "Amy and Joseph Mann" are both valid options. If a bride is choosing to retain her maiden name, the couple may choose to be introduced by their full individual names, such as "Amy Kennedy and Joseph Mann." They may also be introduced by their first names only, which is typically more informal, but also an option.

 **Essential**

While it is not a necessity, your parents will be honored if you choose to introduce them alongside the wedding party during the grand entrance. In fact, in some cultures, grandparents, godparents, and sponsors are all a part of the grand entrance.

## The Send-Off

**What is the send-off?** It is the formal exit of the newlyweds. A formal send-off is not mandatory, but it does provide a definitive conclusion to the event. Depending on the rules of the venue, guests may shower the couples with rose petals, bubbles, or light sparklers for the exit. Another option is to have the emcee play a last dance song and gather the guests on the dance floor. At some point toward the middle of the song, the emcee cues you to exit and the guests are left to finish the dance while you head on out.

## Cheers!

Clink! Clink! Cheers! The wedding toasts can be memorable, bringing tears to your eyes and a smile to your face. Toasts should be no longer than a few minutes and should not involve inside jokes or anything too personal. Create a list of those who are to propose a toast and pass it along to the planner or emcee so that your wedding doesn't become open mic night.

## The Toasts

**Who makes the first toast?** The best man traditionally makes the first toast. His toast should take place toward the beginning of the evening, following the grand entrance or near the time the first course is served.

**My maid of honor wants to propose a toast. Is this okay?** Toasting is no longer for the best man alone. It is quite common for the maid of honor to have her turn at the microphone. Her toast should follow the best man's.

**What are we supposed to do while we are being toasted?** The main thing to remember is that people are making a toast to you; therefore, at the conclusion of the toast, you should not drink to yourselves. During the toast, be attentive and smile. If the emcee asks the guests to rise for the toast, the bride and groom should remain seated.

 **Fact**

If you have scheduled many toasts for your wedding reception, spread them throughout the evening. For example, have your father welcome the guests, begin the meal service, then have the best man and maid of honor propose their toasts. Other toasting can be done throughout the meal, concluding with the bride and groom's toast at the cake cutting.

## Pass the Mic

**Should my father propose a toast?** This toast is completely optional, but if your father would like to propose a toast, it should be scheduled after the best man has his go at the microphone. In some cases, the father of the bride, as host of the event, welcomes the guests. In this case, he should speak at the beginning of the reception, before the best man.

**Do the bride and groom have to propose a toast?** It is not mandatory, but at some point during the reception the guests expect and would love to hear from the bride and groom.

## Toasting Order

**Many of my attendants and family members want to propose a toast. Is there a correct order to follow?** The following list of toasting order is extensive and inclusive; not everyone on the list needs to or will want to propose a toast. Other than the best man's toast, all others are optional. Parents often combine their toasts rather than offering separate ones. If there is a blessing or prayer to be offered it should be offered prior to any toasts.

**Toasting Order**
- Best man
- Groom toasts the bride
- Maid of honor
- Bride toasts the groom
- Father of the bride toasts the couple
- Bride toasts the groom's parents
- Groom toasts the bride's parents
- Father of the groom toasts the bride
- Father of the bride toasts the groom
- Mother of the bride toasts the couple
- Mother of the groom toasts the couple

# May I Have This Dance?

The special dances at the wedding reception are sweet moments in time. There is nothing quite like your first dance as husband and wife or sharing a dance with your father.

## The First Dance

**When do we do the first dance?** Traditionally, no one should take the dance floor until the bride and groom have danced their first dance. There are many opportunities to do the first dance earlier in the reception so that your guests can feel free to get up and dance if the mood strikes them. A very popular option is to do the first dance immediately following the grand entrance; as the bride and groom enter the venue, they go directly to the dance floor and right into their dance. It may also be done between courses or as the meal concludes.

**My fiancé and I already take dance lessons, but we specialize in salsa dancing. Would a salsa be appropriate for a first dance?** The style of your wedding would dictate whether or not a salsa number is appropriate. If you are having a Latin-themed wedding or a more eclectic mix of traditions, a salsa could work as a first dance. For a more formal or traditional reception, a salsa may not be the right choice for a first dance, but that doesn't mean you cannot fit it in somewhere else. Plan to surprise your guests with a salsa dance later in the evening, possibly even slipping into different attire to really set the mood.

## Dancing the Night Away

**When is the father/daughter dance done?** The father/daughter dance is the second dance of the evening, but it doesn't necessarily need to follow the first dance immediately. For example, if the first dance followed the grand entrance, the father/daughter dance can be held after the first course is served or once the meal concludes.

**Fact**

The order for protocol dancing is as follows: first dance, father/daughter, mother/son, bride's/groom's parents, bride with her father in-law, groom with his mother-in-law, and the bridesmaids and ushers dance with each other. Then open dancing begins. Of course, you may exclude some or all of these dances.

**My father will not be at my wedding. How do I address the father/daughter dance?** You need not make any mention of the dance at all, just pass it by and no one will even notice. As an alternative, you can ask whoever is walking you down the aisle, or a brother, special friend, family member, or even your new father-in-law to dance with you.

**I'm close to both my father and stepfather. With whom should I dance the father-daughter dance?** This depends entirely upon your relationships with your natural father and stepfather, and you should discuss this with both men prior to making a decision. Consider beginning the dance with your natural father and having your stepfather cut in or doing two separate dances. If you're really in a quandary, you can dispense with the father-daughter dance altogether.

## Let Them Eat Cake

The cake cutting is a lovely tradition that can quickly turn ugly. Everyone has seen the images of a bride and groom smashing cakes into each other faces. Really, no one wants to walk around with cake up their nose. So take the dignified route. Make a pact to have a classy cake cutting that the guests will remember for all the right reasons.

## Cutting the Cake

**When do we cut the cake?** The cake cutting is done about an hour after the meal service concludes. However, in recent years, couples have switched things up. Some couples like cutting the cake between courses of the meal and some couples cut the cake immediately following the meal. It really depends on personal preference. Just don't put it off for too long, as it is considered rude for guests to leave before the cake is cut.

**What is the proper way to cut the cake?** You and your groom usually cut the first piece together. Place your right hand on the knife, and he should place his hand over yours. Place a small piece on a plate and then the groom feeds the bride a small bite, followed by the bride doing the same to the groom. The caterer or baker then cuts the rest of the cake and distributes it to guests.

## A Cake of His Own

**What is a groom's cake and do we need one?** The groom's cake, a long-standing Southern tradition that has become popular throughout the country, is a reflection of the groom, both in flavor and style. The cake, usually smaller than the wedding cake, can be decorated with team logos and colors or to reflect the groom's hobbies or interests. Chocolate is the traditional flavor, but it's okay to let the groom pick a different flavor. It can be displayed alongside the wedding cake or on its own table.

## Toss It!

The single guests either revel in the traditions of tossing the garter and bouquet or cringe at the thought of being singled out at this celebration of love and marriage. Of course, legend has it that the man who catches the garter is to be the next groom, and the woman who catches the bouquet is to marry next. These activities are entirely optional, so you may choose to modify them, skip them, or come up with something new that better suits your style.

## The Bouquet

**Do I have to toss my bouquet?** Including or excluding this tradition is totally up to you. If you do choose to toss the bouquet, the bride rarely, if ever, tosses her original bridal bouquet. If you are planning to toss a bouquet, ask the florist to make you a toss bouquet; these are usually included at little to no charge. These bouquets are small and made specifically for the toss so that the bride may keep her own.

 **Essential**

If you are on the fence about tossing your bouquet, consider dedicating it to someone special in a show of love and appreciation. Your mother, grandmother, your new mother-in-law, or a special family friend are possible recipients. Present the lady with the bouquet and say a few heartfelt words about why she means so much to you.

**Can you throw the bouquet without tossing the garter?** Of course! If you feel uncomfortable with the garter toss, as many brides do, it's perfectly acceptable to eliminate that tradition while keeping the bouquet toss.

## The Garter

**When do we do the garter toss?** Like the bouquet toss, the garter toss is optional. It is usually done later in the reception, around the same time as the cake cutting. Work with the wedding planner and entertainment to find the right time to toss the garter.

# New Ways to Wed

The creativity and ingenuity of couples and wedding professionals have helped to create new, fun, and memorable ideas that add sparkle and pizzazz to modern weddings. Surprise and delight are in store for your guests when you mix things up. Add some personal touches, incorporate meaningful elements, and possibly create a tradition all your own.

## The Marriage of Ideas

**I want to have a guestbook, but not a traditional one. What are couples doing for their guestbooks now?** Guestbooks are traditional and full of priceless wedding memories. If you want something less traditional, try a photo guestbook, where an instant photo is snapped of the guests as they enter the reception and is immediately placed in the guest book, where the guest writes his or her well wishes right next to the photo. You can also ask guests to sign a beautiful coffee table–style book that represents something to you or about your wedding, such as a book filled with photos of your honeymoon destination. Another idea that has been popular for quite a while is a framed engagement photo, where guests sign their well wishes on the photo matte. The framed photo can be hung in your home.

 **Fact**

Favors aren't necessary, but are a tradition that most couples continue to embrace. If you are giving something edible, like a piece of chocolate or cookies, plan on one favor per person. If you are giving something like a picture frame or a candle, one per couple or family is fine. It is great for the favor to have meaning to you or your fiancé, such as your favorite candies, or something related to the destination of the wedding.

## Lasting Ideas

**It seems everyone is talking about signature drinks. What do they mean by this?** A signature drink is an alcoholic or non-alcoholic beverage that the bride and groom helped create or drink regularly, or a drink that reflects the wedding theme. Creating a signature drink has become a new tradition that brides and grooms seem to love.

## Going Green

**I think the best tradition I can start is being eco-friendly. How can I go green at my wedding?** Going green is a trend that will turn into a wedding staple. Here are some ideas to make your wedding green:

- Ask the caterer, venue, and guests to recycle.
- Use locally grown organic produce, products, and flowers.
- Use potted plants (that can later be planted) for table decor.
- Use paper-free invitations or use 100 percent post-consumer waste recycled paper and nontoxic inks.
- Serve organic wines.
- Have your favors reflect a green theme. Give guests reusable shopping bags, stainless steel water bottles, tree seedlings, seeds, or organic fruits.
- For typically disposable items such as table numbers and escort/place cards, use organic items such as leaves, lemons, and rocks, use reusable products such as photo frames, and choose accessories that are made from recycled paper.

# CHAPTER 16

# The Wedding Puzzle

*T*hat magical day that seemed as though it was eons away is right around the corner. Your plans are in place, but they look like a wedding-planning puzzle. The pieces are there but how do they fit together? Don't fret! As you prepare for the wedding day, a little reorganization is in order. Call your vendors, create a timeline, go shopping, and take a little time for yourself. Before you know it, the pieces will fall into place, and your vision will come to life.

## The Wedding-Day Itinerary

Where to go, how to get there, and when to be there—essential information that the wedding party, your parents, and the vendors all need to know. As the wedding day approaches, not only do you have paperwork to fill out and timelines to plan, but most importantly, you need to communicate this to all of the involved parties. A well-planned itinerary is the ideal way to do this.

**How do I create my wedding-day itinerary?** The following steps highlight the information you should include when developing a wedding-day itinerary:

- Begin with the established start times of the ceremony and reception and work forward and backward to fill in the schedule.
- Confirm arrival and setup times with the ceremony and/or reception venues.

- Schedule departure and arrival times, being sure to account for travel time to and from all locations.
- Schedule pre-ceremony events, such as hair and makeup and photo sessions.
- Confirm arrival and departure times with the vendors.
- Create a schedule for photography.
- Determine which traditions will be incorporated into the ceremony and reception.
- Confirm and review the timing for the formalities (grand entrance, toast, first dance, etc.) with the location manager and the entertainment.
- Include detailed information on décor and setup plans.
- Include wedding-day contact names and office and cell phone numbers for all vendors.

## Vendor Confirmation

After planning so carefully and spending so much money to create the perfect wedding day, now is not the time to let any details slip through the cracks. As the day draws nearer, calling and e-mailing each vendor to finalize details, including the wedding-day itinerary, will provide you with peace of mind and assure you that your wedding plans are right on track.

### Paperwork

**How do I know when I need to pay the vendors and return the paperwork?** Go through your signed contracts and paperwork and make a calendar showing when each vendor needs his payments and any necessary paperwork. Among other things, the DJ or band needs your list of musical selections, the caterer needs a guest count, and the baker needs what cake flavors you have finally decided upon.

## Follow Up

**How should I follow up and confirm the details with my vendors?** As the big day gets closer, you should contact each vendor to confirm the details. At this point, a phone call is in order. In addition, each vendor should be supplied with a hard copy of the itinerary (sent via fax or e-mail) to be sure everyone knows the plan on the wedding day. Of course, if you make any changes to your services or products, there should be written confirmation.

# Picture Perfect

Your wedding photos will be with you for a lifetime—every fantastic moment captured on film. A good working relationship with your photographer is instrumental in capturing the enduring images of your wedding. After you have put your time into researching a quality photographer, it is also important to prepare yourself and your fiancé to look your best so that these photos bring a smile to your face forever.

## The Photographer

**What should we look for when selecting a photographer?** Do you want a more photojournalistic approach, which documents the day as it unfolds with less posing and more spontaneity? Or do you prefer a more traditional style of photography that includes more poses, utilizes lighting, and sets up shots? Some photographers offer an editorial approach so that it almost seems as though you are posing for a magazine spread. There are a host of photographers who mix all of these approaches to create their own unique style. Decide on a style, then hire a photographer you like. He will be with you much of the day, and he should be someone you feel comfortable with. Finally, you should decide whether you have a preference regarding film or digital images.

**Does it matter if the photographer shoots digital or film?** While film was once highly preferred, high-end digital equipment can provide nearly the same quality. Some couples love the look of film and some want the flexibility of digital. Each type of photography has pros and cons, and ultimately you should not count out either style until you find the photographer you want to hire.

## Capture the Moment

**Should we provide our photographer with a checklist of important photos?** Most professional wedding photographers know what photos they need to take and what photos a couple expects. However, it does not hurt to make a list outlining your expectations. Must-have photos typically include you and your groom, both of you with your families (parents, grandparents, siblings), the wedding party, and the important moments of the ceremony and reception. You may want to ask the photographer to get some "behind the scenes" shots as you finish getting ready. Another photo opportunity is of the wedding décor and environment itself since you spent so much time and effort designing this aspect of the wedding.

## Preparing for the Wedding Day

You've planned, you've confirmed, and you've planned some more. All that's left to do is get married—or so it seems. There are some final preparations for the wedding day that still need to be tended to. So get going! There are things to pack, copies to make, and places to go.

## A Place for Everything

**I have a lot of wedding accessories. Do I just bring them with me on the wedding day?** First, sort the accessories; put the ceremony items together and the reception items together so there is no question about where anything should be. Then, ask your wedding planner if she will be responsible for delivering the items to the correct venue. If so, drop them off at her office one to two days prior to the wedding. If you do not have a wedding planner, ask the location manager at the ceremony and reception venues if there is a secure room where these items can be stored and drop the items off there prior to the wedding day. If neither of these options works out, ask a (very) trustworthy friend to take charge of this task.

 **Essential**

Amenity baskets, filled with aspirin, hairspray, mouthwash, mints, shoe shine towels, bobby pins, and other necessities can be placed in the reception restrooms and are a great treat for the guests. It shows you are trying to take care of the guests' every need, just as a good host should.

## Wedding-Day Accessories

**What wedding accessories do I need for my wedding?**
Each wedding differs in design and style. Your particular wedding may have more or fewer accessories than those listed here. Add in specialty items, check them off, and you are ready for the wedding day.

### Wedding Accessory Checklist
- ❑ Aisle runner
- ❑ Bubbles, rose petals, etc.
- ❑ Cake knife/server
- ❑ Cake topper
- ❑ Cash and envelopes (extra)
- ❑ Card box
- ❑ Centerpieces
- ❑ Copies of itinerary, vendors' contracts, vendor contact numbers, seating chart

❑ Decorations
❑ Disposable table cameras
❑ Escort/Place cards
❑ Favors
❑ Flower girl basket
❑ Guest book and pen
❑ Ring pillow
❑ Table numbers
❑ Toasting flutes
❑ Unity candle
❑ Wedding programs

# CHAPTER 17

# The Best Laid Plans

*N*o matter how much you plan and prepare, you cannot control everything and everyone. Chances are there will be a mishap here or a misstep there on your wedding day. And guess what? Most of these snafus can be easily fixed and the guests will never even notice. So don't get obsessed with wedding perfection. Have fun, relax, and remember that it is not about planning a wedding—it is about getting married.

## All Dressed Up and . . . Whoops!

Groomsmen forget black socks, buttons fall off, stockings run, and zippers stick. There is no telling what may happen when everyone is all dressed up with some place to go. While the attire can be the cause of many last-minute glitches on the wedding day, these situations are easily handled if you have the right "tools" on hand.

### Dressing Issues

**It is three months until my wedding, the bridesmaids' dresses have been ordered, and one of my bridesmaids just told me she is two months pregnant. The dress surely won't fit when she is five months pregnant. What should I do?** After congratulating your friend, your next step is to call the bridal salon and see if it is still possible to order a larger size or a maternity size or style for your friend. You may have to pay for two dresses at this point. You can also ask if the manufacturer will sell yardage of the dress fabric. If so, a good seamstress will be able to either make you a new dress in a flattering maternity style or possibly alter the dress, with the addition of side panels, so that it will fit.

## Don't Forget . . .

**My fiancé's friends are great but a little absent-minded. I am afraid they are going to forget the essentials, like black socks, on the wedding day. What can I do to prevent this?** Men, especially those who do not go to work in a suit and tie, don't always realize what it takes to get dressed to the nines. Put together a checklist of essential items to remember for the groomsmen and the bridesmaids, and e-mail it to everyone at least one week prior to the wedding.

# It's a Bridal Emergency!

You're moments away from walking down the aisle and you need double-stick tape to keep a hem up and a mint to get rid of dragon breath. You can avoid disaster with a well-stocked emergency kit. This is one wedding accessory that no bride should be without. A carefully packed kit that includes simple everyday items and wedding-specific items is a lifesaver for you and your guests.

## The Kit

**Why and what should I pack in an emergency kit?** The emergency kit is not only for the wedding party; it is really for everyone at the wedding. When you have 150 guests, you never know when someone might need some antacid or some aspirin.

## The Bridal Emergency Kit Checklist

**What should be in a bridal emergency kit?** The kit should contain essential beauty supplies, toiletries, some office supplies, and pain relievers. It can also be made to accommodate your wedding colors and even the location. For example, if you are marrying on a ranch without a lot of night lighting, flashlights would be an important addition.

- ❑ Aspirin or ibuprofen
- ❑ Baby powder
- ❑ Bobby pins
- ❑ Bottled water
- ❑ Breath mints
- ❑ Cellophane tape
- ❑ Clear bandages or liquid bandage
- ❑ Corsage pins
- ❑ Crackers, energy bars, or other snacks
- ❑ Deodorant
- ❑ Double stick tape
- ❑ Duct tape (one roll of regular and one roll of white)
- ❑ Extra stockings
- ❑ Facial tissue or handkerchief
- ❑ Fabric cleaner
- ❑ Glue
- ❑ Hairspray
- ❑ Money
- ❑ Mouthwash
- ❑ Nail glue
- ❑ Nail polish
- ❑ Rubber bands
- ❑ Sanitary napkins/tampons
- ❑ Scissors
- ❑ Sewing kit (white, black thread, and color-coordinated thread)
- ❑ Spot remover

❑ Static cling spray
❑ Toothbrush and toothpaste
❑ Tweezers
❑ White chalk (for concealing dirt smudges)
❑ White towels (for stain removal)

 **Essential**

After you have packed the main emergency kit, prepare a smaller one just for the groom and his men. He can have it with him in case he has his own emergency, and he won't have to worry about getting a glimpse of (or worrying) you.

## Weather Watch

You have crossed your "t's" and dotted your "i's." Everything on the checklist is accounted for. You are ready for a perfect day. While smooth sailing is the ideal, there are simply some situations you just cannot check off the list, so be prepared in advance and hope for the best.

### Rain

**My fiancé and I want to get married outside, but we are worried about the possibility of rain. What type of backup plan should we have?** There should be a backup plan for any outdoor wedding. Ask the venue what plans they have in place, such as alternate locations on their property (e.g., another event room or a covered patio). Tenting the location is another option, but tents are expensive, so you really have to think about the budget. You should purchase large umbrellas so that the groomsmen can assist the guests to and from their cars.

## Sun

**I am having a summer wedding with an outdoor ceremony. Is there anything I can do so that my guests are not too uncomfortable if it is hot?** You have a few options to help alleviate any discomfort from the heat. Two simple options are to provide plenty of drinking water and invest in hand-held or mini-electric fans. Placing large market umbrellas around the perimeter of the ceremony provides shade for the guests as well. You should also consider having individual umbrellas available for guests to use prior to the ceremony to shade themselves. Just instruct the ushers to ask the guests to not use the umbrellas during the ceremony or to sit in the back row if they must use them. Tenting is another solution, but it is also more expensive.

 **Fact**

You should never leave the guests waiting, but that is all the more important if the guests are in an uncomfortable situation such as severe heat and/or direct sun. In such circumstances, don't seat the guests until just before you are ready to begin, and most importantly, start the ceremony on time!

## Last-Minute Whoopsies

The perfect white gown may get dirty. Flowers may wilt. A button may fall off. A vendor may be caught in a traffic jam. No matter how carefully you've planned, these are the things that will keep you up at night wondering, "what if . . . ." Unfortunately, you can't see these last-minute whoopsies coming, but solving the problem and moving on when and if they happen will be easy if you are prepared.

## The Gown

**What if I stain or rip my gown on my wedding day?** As part of your bridal emergency kit, you should include specific items for gown repair. Ask your bridal salon which cleaner should be used to clean emergency stains from your wedding gown; special garments require special care. Don't forget to include white towels to blot with and hold behind the stain while you clean it, a sewing kit, white chalk, and white powder.

## The Wedding Rings

**What if we forget the wedding rings?** For the bride, simply use the engagement ring as a stand-in for the real ring. For the groom, fake it, and when the time comes, smile, relax, and do your best acting job. You can also use a stand-in such as one of your fathers' rings.

## Vendors

**What should I do if I have a problem with a vendor on the day of the wedding?** The "what if" scenario is probably the best argument for hiring a wedding planner; she will have years of experience in dealing with vendor problems, and if something does go wrong, she can take care of it. Also, make sure your contract includes a clause that states that if goods are not delivered as stipulated in the contract, you will get a full refund of your deposit.

Be sure your wedding planner or a trusted friend has a copy of the itinerary and contact numbers for each vendor. She can call the vendors to check on their progress if there are any delays with their arrival or services. Also, bring your copies of the contracts to have on site, just in case there are any questions about the service details.

## Headaches and Heartbreaks

Unfortunately, not all problems are the result of poor planning or misguided wedding professionals. Some problems, especially those involving feuding families, cannot be predicted. There is no single correct answer to any question regarding family difficulties; it all depends upon family history and the dynamics of a particular situation. If you suspect a problem is on the horizon, be proactive, discuss your concerns, and make a plan about what to do in case any tensions flare up or an unexpected tragedy occurs.

## D-I-V-O-R-C-E

**What can I do if my husband's ex-wife shows up at the church uninvited?** If you think she intends to cause a scene, alert your ushers to this possibility ahead of time so that when she arrives they can quietly ask her to leave. You can also ask a relative or close friend to be a point person in this situation, keeping post at the door to head her off.

## Cordially Uninvited

**I uninvited my brother to the wedding, and I am afraid he is going to show up anyway. What can I do to make sure he doesn't ruin my day?** Short of hiring security, which is actually an option if you are very concerned, you will have to ask your grooms-men or other reliable friends to keep an eye out for him and ask him to leave. You and your fiancé need to find others to help you with this so that you don't end up in an argument on the church steps with your brother. Be sure to let your venue and wedding planner know what is happening; they may be able to assist too.

**We have friends of friends that were not invited to the wedding but they keep talking as if they are coming. What do I do if they show up?** First, ask your mutual friends to help you out by tactfully mentioning to the other couple that they are not invited. You may also choose to be more direct and talk to them yourself, confirming they are not invited. If they do show up, have someone talk to them and explain they are not on the guest list and there is not a seat for them.

## Let's Call the Whole Thing Off

In some cases, you may never even get to your wedding day. You and your fiancé may have made the difficult and painful decision that you would both be better off if you didn't get married. Worse yet, an illness or death may leave you needing to postpone the wedding. Whatever the circumstances, there are some guidelines to follow if your wedding plans change.

### Postponed

**My brother is seriously ill. He wants us to go ahead with the wedding if he dies, but I don't think this is proper. What should I do?** Every situation is unique and should be treated as such. Thoughtful discussions with your families and clergy may be in order to finalize any decisions. In this circumstance, you should feel comfortable proceeding with the wedding in accordance with your brother's wishes. A poem, song, or Scripture reading during the ceremony could honor his memory, as could a toast at the reception. Toning down the jovial atmosphere and the music at your reception may be in order as well.

**What is the etiquette for postponing a wedding?** If the invitations have been printed and not yet mailed, you may include a printed card stating the new date, such as "The wedding date has been changed from April 12 to June 18." If necessary, it is even okay to neatly cross out the date on the invitation and write in the correct one. If the invitations have already been mailed, a new announcement recalling the first invitation and stating the new date or the fact that the wedding has been postponed should be printed and mailed. A round of phone calls and e-mails can give your guests a heads-up on the change so they may adjust their travel plans.

## Cancelled

**My fiancé and I are calling off the wedding. What do I need to do?** The etiquette for cancelling the wedding is the same no matter the reason. If the invitations have not gone out, let your close friends and families know first, either by phone or e-mail (yes, e-mail is acceptable). You can ask your parents for help in this matter. If you sent Save-the-Dates, you may need to expand this phone/e-mail list to include your entire guest list, especially if some guests will already be busy making travel plans. A card can be sent if there is enough time. As for the ring and the gifts, they need to be returned. After you have notified the guests, you will need to let your vendors know as well. Additionally, a short announcement should be sent to the newspaper that carried the original engagement announcement.

 **Fact**

To notify the guests of a cancellation, send cards stating "Mr. and Mrs. Grant Nelson/announce that the marriage of their daughter/Carolyn Rachel/to/Eric Stephen Martin/will not take place." If time is at a premium, you and your ex-fiancé should phone your guests to tell them personally.

## Keep It? Return It?

**Should I keep my engagement ring or give it back to my fiancé?** The ring should be returned to whoever purchased it, typically the man. However, some may argue that if the man broke the engagement, the woman is entitled to keep the ring. If the ring was a joint purchase, you will need to decide how to dispose of the ring and potentially split the profits. If the ring was an heirloom, it should be returned to the family of origin.

**What should we do with the engagement or wedding gifts we've already received?** You should return all gifts to their senders along with a note thanking them for their kindness but explaining that the wedding will not take place. This includes all gifts that have been monogrammed. If you received any checks or cash, you should send the money back as well. And if you jumped the gun a bit and already started using some of your wedding gifts, buy replacements and send them back. Under no circumstances should you send a used gift back to the sender.

# CHAPTER 18

# When the Party's Over

*W*ith all the frenzied coordinating, organizing, and worrying involved, getting yourself married can be a full-time job—and then some! Fortunately, your honeymoon, a once-in-a-lifetime trip, is the grand finale of your wedding and the reward for your careful planning. Once you get back, it is time to start living life as a married couple. But before you jump right into married life, there are a few wedding-related tasks left to tackle.

## Countdown to Paradise

Ten years from now, you probably won't recall just when it was you spent that week in the mountains, or that long weekend skiing. But you're bound to remember nearly every detail about your honeymoon. On the surface, a honeymoon is no different from any other vacation you might take, but to a pair of newlyweds, the honeymoon is a much-anticipated getaway.

 **Alert**

> Be sure to make travel arrangements for your honeymoon under your maiden name. You will not have a passport or driver's license in your married name yet, and it is imperative that you are able to present the proper documentation and ID to travel.

**My fiancé and I are at our wit's end. He likes to ski, I like to sunbathe. What should we do?** Arguing about where to take your honeymoon almost defeats the purpose. This is your time to enjoy each other's company, relax, and experience the ultimate vacation. The time of year may dictate what type of honeymoon you take anyway, so check into weather conditions in the destinations you are considering. Most importantly, you and your fiancé need to find a middle ground. Perhaps, with compromise, you can schedule a week at a beachfront resort to follow the wedding and a ski vacation in six months, or vice versa.

## Tipping While Traveling

The questions of when, whom, and how much to tip are a part of traveling. Travelers often feel embarrassed or confused about this issue, so do some research before you leave for your honeymoon. It is better to begin your journey with some knowledge of the travel tipping structure. Once you are at your destination, you can ask the hotel management what is standard or consult a guidebook. In some cases, such as cruises, the destination provides you with tipping etiquette.

### Hotels and Resorts

**What is considered standard when tipping hotel staff?** Standard amounts are as follows:

- **Bellboy:** $1 per bag, plus $1 for hospitable gestures—turning on lights, opening windows. Tip on service.
- **Chambermaid:** $1 for each service, minimum $5 per couple per week. Tip each day; a new chambermaid may be assigned during your stay.
- **Doorman:** $1 per bag; $1 for hailing a taxi. Tip on service.
- **Headwaiter:** $5 per week for special service, $2–$3 for regular service. Tip on your first day.

- **Wait staff:** 15 to 20 percent of the bill when no service charge is added; some add 5 percent when there is a service charge. Tip at each meal.
- **Room service:** 15 to 20 percent of bill in addition to room service charge. If menu or bill explicitly states that a gratuity will automatically be added, you might add an additional $1 or refrain from tipping altogether.
- **Other service personnel:** The general rule is to tip 15 to 20 percent of the bill, unless the person serving you owns the business. They may not accept tips but may charge more for their exclusive services.

 Question

**What is the going rate for tipping at the airport?**
Tip the porter at the airport $1 per bag when you check in at the curb or have bags taken to check in for you. If the luggage is heavy, tip a little more. Obviously, if you go the DIY route, no tip is necessary or expected.

## Cruising

**What's the tipping etiquette on a cruise ship?** The staff on each cruise line can outline tipping etiquette and procedures for their ship. Some ships are "no tip" ships, some automatically add a gratuity to the bill, and others practice person-to-person tipping, in which case each staff person is presented with an envelope on the last night of the cruise. The following will give you a good idea of what to expect in terms of tipping amounts:

- **Room steward:** $3.50 per day per person. Tip at the end of the trip.
- **Dining room waiter and busboy:** Waiter, $3.50 per person per day, half that for the busboy.

- **Maitre d' and headwaiter:** Seventy-five cents per day, per guest.
- **Bartenders, wine steward, pool and deck attendants, etc.:** On almost all ships, a service charge is automatically added to the bar bill, making a tip unnecessary. Be sure to check.
- **Other service personnel** should be tipped when the service is given, at the same rate as for service ashore, usually 15 percent.

 **Fact**

Many ships have a "tipping not required" policy, emphasizing that tips are at the passenger's discretion. Other ships have implemented a daily gratuity charge of anywhere from $5 to $10 per day per guest that is automatically charged to the passenger's account. Bar and alcohol charges are typically not included in these amounts.

## Gifts: The Good, the Bad, and the Ugly

Your wedding gifts will probably start trickling in soon after you send out your first wedding invitations. As you get closer and closer to your wedding date, this trickle turns into a steady stream, and it is exciting to come home from a hard day at the office and open a beautiful package. Most guests will shop from your registry, but there are always some who choose to send you whatever they think you need or would like, no matter how offbeat that is.

### Protecting the Gifts

**How can we ensure that gifts brought to the reception will be safe?** Generally, guests should send gifts to the bride's home. However, many guests do bring gifts to the reception, so you should ask a trusted friend or relative to act as a gift attendant, keeping watch over the gift table. Once the reception is in full swing, she should lock the gifts in a secure room. Also, if the reception is in a hotel, lock any money envelopes in the hotel's safe deposit box. If you're leaving for your honeymoon straight from the reception, have someone take the gifts from the reception site to your home.

**Can we exchange duplicate wedding gifts?** Of course, but it's a good idea to wait until you've received most or all of your presents before you begin exchanging them; you don't want to exchange a toaster for a cappuccino maker only to get another cappuccino maker a week later. Also, some duplicate gifts are worth keeping—you can always use a few extra glasses or another set of towels.

## Not-So-Perfect Gifts

**What if we've received gifts that we don't care for?** This is a very tricky issue. On one hand, what on earth are you going to do with an oil painting of your uncle's horse? On the other hand, how can you possibly get rid of it when the sender is your fiancé's favorite uncle who stops by once a month? In this case, the easiest solution would be to keep it accessible and take it out whenever this uncle comes over. In cases where the sender is not such a frequent visitor, you can probably get away with returning the gift in question for something a little more in keeping with your taste.

**What do we do if we receive damaged gifts?** If the gift came through the mail and was insured, let the person who sent it know so that he or she can collect the insurance money. If the gift was not insured or did not come through the mail, try to find the store where the gift was bought and exchange it; don't tell the sender that the gift was damaged. If you're not sure what store the gift came from, try to discreetly find out from the sender where the gift was purchased.

# Thank You! Thank You!

Even in today's world of instant communication, handwritten personalized thank-you notes are one rule of etiquette that's here to stay. While everyone appreciates the gift, almost everyone dreads the thought of writing dozens upon dozens of thank-you notes. However, it is imperative to express your gratitude to the sender of every gift, whether it is the perfect addition to your china cabinet or a velvet oil painting of a rabbit.

## What to Say

**What is the proper way to write a thank-you note?** The basics of thank-you notes are actually quite simple. Mention the gift, how you plan to use it, and thank the guest for their generosity. You might write something like, "Thank you so much for the lovely wine glasses. They are the perfect addition to our bar set. We are looking forward to your next visit. We have a special bottle of wine to share with you. We are so glad you were able to be with us at our wedding." If the gift is monetary, write something like, "Thank you so much for the generous gift. It will truly help us in completing our set of formal china. We appreciate your thoughtfulness. We are so glad you were able to be with us at our wedding."

## Getting It Done

**Can my fiancé write thank-you notes?** Since the wedding gifts are given to both of you, it is absolutely appropriate for your fiancé to do his fair share of the note writing. What's more, his friends and relatives would most likely appreciate seeing a note from him personally.

**Should I send thank-yous to our officiant and vendors?** Everyone who assisted in making your wedding day memorable should be honored with a thank-you note. That includes not only your officiant, but your wedding vendors and any family members and friends who may have contributed their time, effort, and expertise.

 **Alert**

Some brides think they have up to a year after the wedding to send a thank-you note. The fact is that while wedding guests have up to a year to bestow a gift upon you and your honey, you have at most three months (sooner is always better) to come back with a thank-you note.

**If I received a group gift, do I need to send thank-you notes to everyone?** If five coworkers chipped in to buy you one nice gift, five separate thank-you notes aren't necessary. Just one, sent to your office, will suffice. However, if five cousins who live in different parts of the country sent you one gift from all of them, send each of them a note.

## To Change or Not to Change

For years, you may have taken your own surname for granted, but faced with its possible loss, you may find yourself more attached to the name than you realized. This is the name you went through school with, the name you went to work with, the name everyone knows you by. It feels like a part of you. On the other hand, maybe your last name is ten syllables long, no one can ever pronounce or spell it right, and you can't wait to get rid of it.

### The Decision

**For professional reasons, I don't want to abandon my own name completely. What are my options?** Lucky for you, when it is time to change your name there are options:

- Use your maiden name as your middle name and your husband's as your last. So if Jennifer Andrews married Trevor Miller, she'd be Jennifer Andrews Miller.
- Hyphenate the two last names: Jennifer Andrews-Miller. This means that the two separate last names are now joined to make one name (kind of like a marriage). You keep your regular middle name, but saying your full name can be a mouthful: Jennifer Marie Andrews-Miller.
- Take your husband's name legally, but use your maiden name professionally. In everyday life and social situations, you'd use your married name, but in the office, you'd use the same name you always had.
- Hyphenate both your and your husband's last names: Jennifer Andrews-Miller and Trevor Andrews-Miller.

## Make It Legal

**How do I make my name change official?** Before you can make any official changes to your name, you will need to have a copy of your certified marriage license. Then you can download forms from the Internet and begin the process. Among other things, you will need a new social security card and legally valid form of identification, usually a driver's license.

**Who needs to be notified of my name change?** If one or both of you will be changing your name after marriage, you should be sure to update the following:

- Bank accounts (savings, checking, 401(k) plans, investment accounts, etc.)
- Car registrations
- Credit cards
- Driver's license
- Employment records
- Insurance policies
- Internal Revenue Service records

- Leases
- Passport
- Pension plan records
- Post office listings
- Property titles
- School records or alumni listings
- Social Security
- Stock certificates
- Utility and telephone information
- Voter registration
- Will

 **Essential**

Name-change kits are widely available and provide the proper forms and information you need to legally change your name. Each state has its own requirements, so be sure to purchase a kit that is customized for your state.

## Stating Your Preference

**I have decided not to change my name. What do I do when someone incorrectly refers to me by my husband's name?** It's an assumption people commonly make unless they know otherwise. You can either let it pass or politely correct the person, depending on how important the issue is to you. To avoid this awkwardness, you may wish to take the initiative and introduce yourself to strangers first: "Hi, I'm Jennifer Andrews, Trevor Miller's wife."

**I'm keeping my maiden name and I'm a little nervous about telling my in-laws for fear of offending them. How should I handle this?** You're right to be sensitive to your in-laws' concerns. Explain the reason for your decision (for example, that you've already established a career identity with your maiden name) and emphasize that your decision in no way reflects a lack of respect for their family. Ask your spouse to voice his support of your decision.

## Get It in Print

Once you are married you will want to announce it to the world, and publishing an announcement in the newspaper or sending an announcement through the mail is a good way to share the news with friends and family.

**Should we send wedding announcements?** Announcements can be useful for spreading the word if you eloped, had a small ceremony, or have many distant relatives who live far away. Announcements should not be sent to anyone who was invited to or attended the wedding. Be selective about who you send them to, however, as wedding announcements can seem like a plea for gifts.

**What is the proper wording for an announcement?** The announcements should include the host's name, couple's names, the date of the wedding, and possibly the location. The following are two samples of wedding announcement wording.

### Announcement Issued by Parents/Hosts

Mr. and Mrs. Jonathan Jones
Have the pleasure of announcing
the marriage of their daughter
Taylor Lynn
to
Michael Allen Nelson
on Saturday, the eleventh of July
Two thousand and twelve
The Glass Chapel
Los Angeles, California

### Announcement Issued by the Couple

Taylor Lynn Jones
and
Michael Allen Nelson
announce their marriage
on Saturday, the eleventh of July
Two thousand and twelve
The Glass Chapel
Los Angeles, California

 **Alert**

Wedding announcements should be mailed the day of the wedding. Order your announcements at the same time you order your invitations. Address and prepare them for mailing when you address the wedding invitations so all that needs to be done is to pop them in the mail.

**Should I publish a wedding announcement in the newspaper?** If you published an engagement announcement, it should be followed with a confirmation that the wedding has taken place. Call each publication to obtain their guidelines for printing, fees, and deadlines. Many publications will also print a photo along with the announcement, so be sure to get the specifics on that. The basic announcement should include names, location, and dates. Many couples choose to include additional information such as members of the bridal party, education, work, accomplishments, and honeymoon destination. This can also be a forum to let people know if the bride will be keeping or changing her name.

# CHAPTER 19

# Double Take

*O*nce upon a time, when a bride got married a second time, she and her fiancé were supposed to sneak off to the nearest justice of the peace. Now it's perfectly acceptable for a second-time bride to have any kind of wedding she wants. However, there are issues that will come up as you plan, and you should be considerate and sensitive to those involved in your wedding and your life. On the other hand, maybe your second wedding isn't a remarriage but a vow renewal. Either way, start planning—you have reason to celebrate!

## Announcing the Engagement

**Who should tell my fiancé's children?** Your fiancé should be the one who communicates the happy news to his children. Once the children have been told, you can join in and, together, you can talk with the children about their concerns and how to include them in the planning and the wedding.

 **Fact**

Customarily, engagement announcements are only for the first wedding. Any subsequent marriages would require only a wedding announcement. Spare yourself the extra trouble, unless this is really important to you. If it is, go ahead and announce it.

**Should I let my ex know that I will be getting married again?** Even if you do not have children together, it is only courteous to let your ex know so that he is not shocked when he hears it through the grapevine. If you share children, your ex should be told soon after the children are told. You will need to work out custody arrangements and other issues, and he can then help the children with any feelings they may have.

## Celebratory Soirées

**Can we have an engagement party if we have been married before?** There is no reason you cannot. In fact, most of the events you had for a first wedding are perfectly okay, within reason, for a subsequent trip to the altar.

**Is it proper to have wedding showers or other pre-wedding parties?** If someone from your fiancé's side wants to throw a shower for you, fine, but don't expect anyone from your side of the family to throw you another shower, especially if you had a big one the first time around. Your friends and family should find other ways to celebrate your upcoming marriage, perhaps with a cocktail or dinner party. However, if it is your first marriage but your fiancé's second, then a shower is fine.

## Planning the Event

After you have taken into account the dos and don'ts for a second wedding and considered what feels right for your "old family" and your "new family," you can begin the process of planning the wedding. This wedding can pretty much be whatever you want it to be—big and fancy, cozy and intimate, or totally casual. As an encore bride, you have the option to create a beautiful and meaningful ceremony to celebrate your marriage.

## Attire

**Is it inappropriate for me to wear a white gown?** Lucky for you, pretty much anything goes, and whatever you feel suits you best is what you should select and wear for your wedding. Of course, the gown should match the formality of the wedding and be appropriate for your age and for the location.

**Can I wear a veil and blusher?** While the etiquette is loose for the gown, the issue of the veil is different. A veil that does not cover the face, if it fits with the formality of the wedding, would be fine. You should forego the blusher, as it is a tradition reserved for first-time brides.

## The Ceremony

**Who should give me away?** Who gives you away is completely your decision. It could be your father, but it could also be your children. An eldest son can take on this role, but you can also enter with your groom or simply walk down the aisle alone.

 Alert

Be sure to check with your local county or state about a waiting period after your divorce is legal. It would surely be sad to plan a wedding that cannot officially take place because your county has a waiting period and it is too soon to remarry.

**How can we include our children in the ceremony?** There are many ways to include children and celebrate your union. They can be a part of a unity candle ceremony or a sand ceremony. They can recite a poem or vows written for them. They can also act as attendants.

# Tackling the Issues

If there is anything to be learned from being married before it is that marriage is not all about hearts and flowers and good times. Hopefully your past experiences have given you the knowledge and foresight to realize you need to look out for your best interests. After the ceremony, you will be back to normal, right? But what will normal be now? If either you or your fiancé have children, that normal will involve stepparents, kids, and the blending of finances.

**Is there anything I should do to protect my assets in case something should happen with this marriage?** Only a professional family law attorney can answer specific questions and ensure you are protecting yourself and, more importantly, your children when you remarry, so please consult one in regard to your questions. You may need to consider items such as prenuptial agreements, wills, real estate, credit, spousal support, and custody issues. Get these things in order before you walk down the aisle.

**I am unsure about what to do with my name. Should I leave it so that my children and I have the same name, change back to my maiden name, or take my husband's name?** This is a common question with many possibilities, all affected by each individual situation. One option is to change your name to your new husband's name and deal with explaining the situation when people ask why your children have a different name; in today's world it's likely that no one will even notice. You can also keep your ex's name—at least legally—because it seems to be easier when you and your kids have the same last name. If this is your choice, you can still use your husband's name in social situations. In some rare cases, if the children's father is agreeable to it, you can change your name back to your maiden name and hyphenate it with your ex's name and then change your children's names to reflect this as well.

**How do we decide what my future stepchildren should call me?** Most likely, the children have already met you, and they have probably also decided on what they are going to call you. To avoid any uneasy feelings or confusion from too much change at one time, let the kids go ahead and continue to call you whatever they called you prior to the wedding. If they choose to change that later, discuss it then.

## Reaffirmation and Renewals

When it comes time to celebrate a milestone in your marriage, a vow renewal may be just the thing to do it. Vow renewals typically follow an anniversary of importance or signify the strengthening of your marriage vows after a difficult period in your relationship or life in general. Whatever the reason, it is a beautiful way to celebrate your love and recommitment to one another.

### Renewals

**Is there a difference between a reaffirmation and a vow renewal?** The two are virtually one and the same. A vow renewal or reaffirmation is not a legal act, so there is no need to worry about licenses and legalities. If you would like to do this in a church, you will need to have it approved and sanctioned by the clergy.

### Dos and Don'ts

**Must there be a reason to renew our vows?** You can renew your vows for whatever reason you want, although most couples do it to recognize a milestone in their relationship or a successful outcome of a particularly rough period of time.

**My friend wants to throw me a shower. This seems inappropriate. Am I right, or is she?** Been there, done that. You are not getting married; you are renewing your vows. Your home has been set up and there is no reason for a bridal shower. The same holds true for a bachelorette/bachelor party.

## Invitations

**How do I word an invitation for my vow renewal?** If you are hosting the ceremony, the invitation is worded as follows:

> You are cordially invited
> to the wedding vow renewal of
> Mr. and Mrs. Jonathan Jackson Moore
> Saturday, the twentieth of April
> Two thousand and twelve
> at six o'clock in the evening
> Monterey Beach
> 2511 Ocean Drive
> Monterey, California

## The Guest List

If you or your fiancé have been married before in a big wedding, you know firsthand the problems that can arise in compiling a guest list. Hopefully, you've learned how to deal with your step-parents and how to tell your future in-laws that they can't have twice as many guests as you without offering to pay for them, because a whole new set of challenges awaits you now.

## The Exes

**Should I invite my ex-spouse or ex-in-laws to the wedding?** Generally speaking, ex-spouses and ex-in-laws should not attend your wedding. Even if you think your relationship has evolved to a certain level and you feel okay inviting your ex, you may feel differently when the day comes. Additionally, it can be confusing if you have children together and awkward for many of the guests to see your "old" husband at your "new" wedding.

 **Fact**

Don't feel uncomfortable about inviting friends to join you at your second wedding. Chances are they've given you love and support through your divorce or widowhood. If it's gifts you're worried about, guests aren't under any obligation to buy you gifts for a second wedding.

## The Kids

**My fiancé has a very young son from his previous marriage. Is it okay if he does not attend the wedding?** If the child is young enough that he won't remember the wedding anyway, letting him stay home may not be a problem. But if he's older, he should be there or else he may feel excluded from his father's new life. You can always ask one of his grandparents or another family member to look after him. Of course, check with your fiancé before making any arrangements for his son. It's also a nice gesture to have an older child serve as your honor attendant for your second marriage.

# Index

# We Have EVERYTHING on Anything!

The Everything® list spans a wide range of subjects, with more than 500 titles covering 25 different categories:

| | | |
|---|---|---|
| Business | History | Reference |
| Careers | Home Improvement | Religion |
| Children's Storybooks | Everything Kids | Self-Help |
| Computers | Languages | Sports & Fitness |
| Cooking | Music | Travel |
| Crafts and Hobbies | New Age | Wedding |
| Education/Schools | Parenting | Writing |
| Games and Puzzles | Personal Finance | |
| Health | Pets | |